CULTURES OF THE WORLD®

SOUTH AFRICA

Ike Rosmarin / Dee Rissik

BENCHMARK BOOKS

MARSHALL CAVENDISH
NEW YORK

PICTURE CREDITS
Cover photo: © Bruce Coleman, Inc.
Art Directors & Trip: 20, 28, 34, 50, 56, 57, 58, 70, 82, 86, 96, 124 • Bes Stock: 1, 6, 8, 104, 114 • Susana Burton: 62, 78 • Jan Butchofsky / Houserstock: 5 • Camera Press: 24, 45 • R.J. Harrison-Church: 23, 26 • Andanson James / CORBIS : 102 • Hans Hayden: 54 • Dave G Houser / Houserstock: 53 • Image Bank: 4, 7, 22, 30, 37, 40, 41, 77, 83, 89, 101, 111, 112, 116, 118, 122, 125 • David Keith Jones / Images of Africa: 10, 12, 14, 17, 21, 25, 59, 60, 63, 74, 75, 80, 84, 85, 87, 98, 99, 105, 109, 115, 117 • Bjorn Klingwall: 18, 42, 44, 47, 49, 72, 73, 88, 107, 110 • Life File Photographic Library: 11, 38, 46, 48, 67, 69, 92, 97, 106, 120, 123, 126, 127, 129 • Reuter's Visnews Library: 71 • Ike Rosmarin (South Africa Information Ministry): 16, 19, 27, 31, 39, 68, 121 • Bernard Sonneville: 3, 9, 13, 15, 29, 43, 64, 65, 76, 81, 91, 95, 100, 108 • South Africa-Infoweb: 131 • South Light: 32, 33, 93, 119 • Angelo Tondini / Focus Team Italy: 36, 130 • Topham Picturepoint: 61 • Nik Wheeler: 51, 55, 90

PRECEDING PAGE
A South African Zulu boy. The Zulus are the largest indigenous group in South Africa.

Marshall Cavendish
99 White Plains Road
Tarrytown, NY 10591
Website: www.marshallcavendish.us

© Times Editions Pte Ltd 1996, 1993
© Marshall Cavendish International (Asia) Private Limited 2004
All rights reserved. First edition 1993. Second edition 2004.

® "Cultures of the World" is a registered trademark of Marshall Cavendish Corporation.

Originated and designed by Times Books International
An imprint of Marshall Cavendish International (Asia) Private Limited
A member of the Times Publishing Group

Library of Congress Cataloging-in-Publication Data
Rosmarin, Ike, 1915-
South Africa / by Ike Rosmarin and Dee Rissik.— 2nd ed.
    p. cm. — (Cultures of the world)
Summary: Explores the geography, history, government, economy, people, and culture of South Africa.
Includes bibliographical references (p.) and index.
ISBN 0-7614-1704-4
1. South Africa—Juvenile literature. [1. South Africa.] I. Rissik, Dee, 1953- II. Title. III. Series.
DT1719.R67 2003
968—dc22   2003020923

Printed in China

7 6 5 4 3 2

CONTENTS

The Cape of Good Hope.

A South African woman.

INTRODUCTION

SOUTH AFRICA has a colorful and dramatic history, clouded at times by racial conflict and oppression but also filled with the goodwill of millions of individuals from a wide mix of cultures and beliefs. This has been woven into a unique tapestry that now makes up the Rainbow Nation, as it was named by Nelson Mandela, South Africa's first true president.

The new country, born in 1994 after its first ever democratic elections, has taken its seat at the global table. Having been cut off from most of the world for many years due to apartheid —a policy of racial discrimination by a white minority government over a black majority—the country is now moving ahead under a new government. The state is making new policies that will allow all citizens to share in the wealth of one of the most blessed countries on the African continent. With its abundant natural beauty, its mineral and agricultural wealth, and its drive to right past wrongs, South Africa looks set for a promising future.

GEOGRAPHY

SOUTH AFRICA is located at the southern tip of the African continent. It is bordered by Mozambique and Swaziland to the northeast, Zimbabwe and Botswana to the north, and Namibia to the northwest. The southeastern region of the country surrounds Lesotho. South Africa lies between two oceans: the Indian in the east and the Atlantic in the west. These two oceans meet at the southernmost tip of the country and of the continent, Cape Agulhas.

South Africa has a variety of geographic regions, including mountains, deserts, plateaus, forests, beaches, and rivers. South Africa's position at the tip of Africa and at the junction of the Indian and Atlantic oceans makes it important in world trade.

Left: White sand beach.

Opposite: **Champagne Castle on the Drakensberg range is one of the highest mountains in South Africa.**

LANDSCAPE

South Africa covers a total area of 472,155 square miles (1,222,880 square km), nearly the three times the size of California. There are four main regions: the veld, which refers to open country with grassy patches; the desert areas; the Great Escarpment and highlands; and the coastal region.

Together, the desert areas and the veld form a large plateau in a semicircular shape that occupies the country's interior. The coastal region is a narrow strip fringing the plateau on three sides. Forming a mountainous barrier between the plateau and the coast is the Great Escarpment. It is made up of several mountain ranges that shapes itself into a rocky wall along the eastern and southern edges of the plateau. The Great Escarpment starts near Zimbabwe in the north, and toward the south the Drakensberg range becomes higher and more dramatic. One of South Africa's highest mountains, Champagne Castle, is found in this range and reaches a height of 11,073 feet (3,374 m).

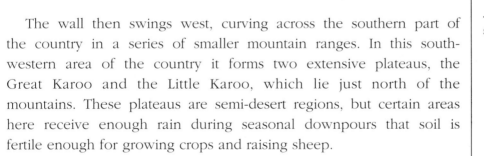

The Atlantic coast of South Africa.

The wall then swings west, curving across the southern part of the country in a series of smaller mountain ranges. In this southwestern area of the country it forms two extensive plateaus, the Great Karoo and the Little Karoo, which lie just north of the mountains. These plateaus are semi-desert regions, but certain areas here receive enough rain during seasonal downpours that soil is fertile enough for growing crops and raising sheep.

In the east, rocky foothills of the Great Escarpment divide the central plateau from the low-lying subtropical region in the Mpumalanga province. A narrow coastal strip of smaller mountains and hills of between about 700 and 1,600 feet (213 and 488 m) above sea level runs along much of the coastline.

Land in the northwest of the country receives very little rainfall and is covered by desert and semi-desert. This area borders the Kalahari Desert, which extends over northern South Africa, Botswana, and Namibia.

Good year-round weather in Western Cape province allows vineyards to be cultivated.

CLIMATE

South Africa suffers from inconsistent rainfall and is often plagued by droughts. Only one-third of the land receives the minimum annual rainfall needed to raise crops. The eastern half of the country is wetter, while much of the west is suitable only for grazing.

In South Africa, the climate varies across the country. In the east summer temperatures average around 75°F (24°C), with daytime highs of 100°F (38°C). The Central area sees average summer temperatures of 66°F (19°C), and daytime highs of 80°F (27°C). Ocean breezes bring the average temperature down to 68°F (20°C) on the southeastern and southern coast, but daytime highs stay in the mid-70s (24°C).

In the winter average temperatures drop to a third of summer's, especially in the higher central areas, but this seldom goes below freezing. In the high regions of the Drakensberg Mountains it is much colder. Snow falls and usually settles for a few weeks almost every winter.

Much of South Africa is located just below the Tropic of Capricorn so the country experiences warm temperatures and a great deal of sunshine.

RIVERS AND LAKES

There are three major rivers in South Africa. The Orange River, the most extensive waterway, is about 1,300 miles (2,092 km) long and flows from Lesotho to the Atlantic Ocean at Alexander Bay. It provides irrigation to the Northern Cape as well hydroelectricity to other parts of the country.

The Vaal River, 750 miles (1,207 km) long, flows west from eastern Mpumalanga and forms part of the border between this province and Free State. The Vaal eventually joins the Orange River in Northern Cape.

The Limpopo River starts near Johannesburg. It is 1,100 miles (1,770 km) long and flows north, then northeast, forming South Africa's border with Zimbabwe. It then cuts through Mozambique and empties into the Indian Ocean.

South Africa's erratic weather causes many small rivers to run dry for long periods. There are few freshwater lakes, but man-made dams have helped to increase water resources for consumption and agriculture. Some marshlands, such as Saint Lucia Lake in KwaZulu-Natal, form during the rainy season.

A river in the Northern Cape province.

Mountain aloe in the Kirstenbosch Botanical Gardens.

FAUNA AND FLORA

Due to the abundance and variety of plant and animal life, South Africa boasts one of the most diverse wildlife displays on Earth. In spite of the wasteful and often needless overkill of game in the 19th century, much of the wildlife has survived. The establishment of the Kruger National Park in 1898 marked the turning point of game conservation across the country.

The country has a very wide variety of game species, including elephants, giraffes, zebras, lions, leopards, hyenas, polecats, badgers, jackals, baboons, monkeys, antelopes, crocodiles, and snakes. Conservation has meant that South Africa still has large herds of elephants as well as good numbers of white rhinoceros and hippopotamus among the many hundreds of other wild animal species.

Ten percent of the planet's known species of birds, including the ostrich and the kori bustard, the heaviest flying bird weighing up to 44 pounds (20 kg), are found here. In the game parks, animals still roam freely in their natural habitat.

NATIONAL PARKS

South Africa has set aside large areas to help preserve its wildlife. In all, there are 20 national parks and 11 declared wilderness areas. The most famous of these is the Kruger National Park, which supports the widest variety of wildlife species on the African continent. The Kruger National Park has an area of more than 7,800 square miles (about 20,000 square km). Numerous roads as well as 24 rest camps with beds, shops, and restaurants have been built within the park to accommodate thousands of visitors. But it is so large that the animals remain undisturbed. It is one of the few places left on Earth where one can observe life in the wild as it must have been thousands of years ago.

The varied climate and lack of rainfall determines much of South Africa's flora. Where rainfall is light, vegetation is poor, and only dry scrub survives. Where rainfall is heavy, palm trees and forests of yellowwood, ironwood, and cedar grow.

Western Cape province has a remarkable collection of spectacular indigenous flowers and shrubs called *fynbos* (f-AY-n-BAWS), Afrikaans for fine bush. The province has 3,000 species and accounts for more than a third of the country's floral kingdom. The national flower, the King Protea, can be found in this province.

Since much of South Africa is grassland, it is not surprising that about 500 species of grass are found in the country.

The major cities have a number of botanical gardens. The most famous is the Kirstenbosch Botanical Gardens in the Cape Town suburbs. More than 25,000 species of plants are grown there. The botanical gardens in Durban have a wide variety of tropical plants because of the hot, humid climate.

Sheep in the hilly country of Langeberg.

REGIONS

After its first democratic elections in 1994, South Africa was divided into nine provinces of varying sizes and population densities. They are:

WESTERN CAPE A Mediterranean climate makes this province suitable for growing crops, especially deciduous fruit and wine grapes.

NORTHERN CAPE Known as diamond country, this is one of the largest provinces but the least populated as most of it is semi-desert. Areas along the Orange River and in the southern sections are fertile and good farming land.

NORTH-WEST This province has fertile soil for growing crops, especially corn. Cattle are also raised here.

EASTERN CAPE The coast in this region offers some of the most beautiful scenery and pristine beaches in the country. Inland it is a good cattle and sheep raising area.

KWAZULU-NATAL The lush subtropical climate in this region is ideal for growing sugarcane. The province has the country's largest Zulu population.

The Jacaranda trees in Pretoria.

FREE STATE Although some areas of this province are fairly dry, it is a good farming area and has large cornfields. It also has some of the country's most productive gold mines.

GAUTENG Although the smallest, this province is the country's economic hub. It has the largest population, the largest city, Johannesburg, and the capital, Pretoria.

MPUMALANGA The fertile lands near the Great Escarpment yield nuts, fruit, and coffee. The region's greatest attraction is the Kruger National Park.

LIMPOPO This province has many provincial and private game reserves, subtropical fruit farms and game ranches It shares international borders with three other African countries: Botswana, Zimbabwe, and Mozambique.

CITIES

South Africa's cities are comparatively young. Modern and well-planned, they are home to more than half South Africa's population.

CAPE TOWN This coastal town nestled next to Table Mountain has a population of 2.9 million. It is the republic's legislative center and an important seaport sitting at the meeting point of major sea routes.

PRETORIA With a population of 1.98 million, South Africa's capital has hilltop government buildings overlooking most of the city.

Pretoria's Church Square.

Johannesburg at night.

JOHANNESBURG Just 28 miles (45 km) south of Pretoria is South Africa's most populous city. Johannesburg has a population of 3.2 million in its metropolitan area. With its large surrounding townships, such as Soweto and others on the eastern side of the city, its overall population is probably closer to 6 million. This vibrant, modern city was founded in 1886 on some of the richest gold deposits in the world. It is often called e'Goli, an African nickname which refers both to the gold mining that led to its founding and its current status as the country's business and economic center.

DURBAN This is the country's second largest city with a population of 3.1 million. It is the largest port in South Africa and the African continent. As such it has developed into a major regional transportation center. Similar to all South Africa's major cities, Durban's population is diverse with a large Indian sector. Because of its subtropical climate and long sandy beaches, it is also an important holiday resort.

PORT ELIZABETH This port city is situated on Algoa Bay and has a population of just over 1 million. It was founded in 1820, when the first British settlers arrived by ship. Today it is an industrial hub with large automobile manufacturing factories. It also handles some of the country's exports of fruit and mineral.

ENVIRONMENT

During the apartheid years, many blacks were forced to live in separate rural areas known as Homelands. Overcrowding, lack of services, and poor environmental awareness caused massive soil erosion in these areas.

The black township of Soweto, an "ecological wasteland."

Forests were destroyed for firewood, and rare animal species faced extinction because of widespread hunting. An overdependence on coal as an energy source caused pollution levels to escalate to dangerous levels. Many international environmental organizations have criticized South Africa for creating "ecological wastelands."

In 1994 a National Reconstruction and Development Program was introduced by the new government. One of its highlights is its emphasis on environmental protection. This is to be achieved by heightening environmental awareness through education. The government is also encouraging small-scale farming in rural areas and ensuring that businesses adhere to international environmental standards.

South Africa's recycling campaigns and pollution control lag behind those in developed countries. Especially in the former Homelands, where many are struggling simply to survive, environmental issues are not a priority. However, the post-apartheid government is attempting to raise the environmental consciousness of South Africans.

Although South Africa is finding new ways to be more environmentally friendly, it will take a while before scenes like this are totally eradicated.

HISTORY

MANY ARCHEOLOGISTS BELIEVE that the prehistoric ancestors of human beings lived in the Sterkfontein caves, about 30 miles (48.3 km) from where Johannesburg is now. The remains of the ape-like beings found here are four million years old and provide clues about the first human inhabitants of South Africa.

One of the earliest known peoples were the San, or Bushmen, who were hunter-gatherers. Many intermarried or settled in communities, but a number remained nomadic hunters in the semi-desert regions of Northern Cape. (They also live in Botswana and Namibia.) Other early immigrants to the southern part of the country included the pastoral Khoikhoi who bred cattle, sheep and goats.

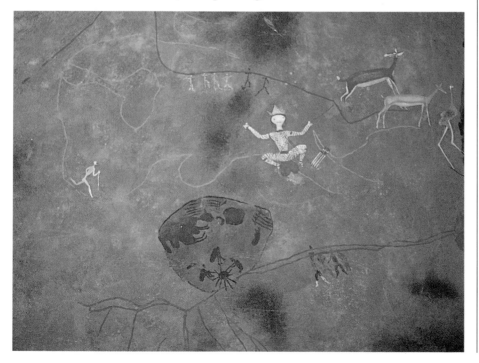

Left: **Bushmen paintings in the Natal National Park.**

Opposite: **The Huguenot Memorial near Franschhoek in Western Cape province.**

THE IRON AGE

The Iron Age inhabitants of South Africa in the 11th and 12th centuries were very likely the ancestors of the black South Africans of today.

The first black immigrants to South Africa were the Sotho, Nguni, Tsonga, and Venda from central Africa. By the 14th century, the Nguni occupied large areas in KwaZulu-Natal and Eastern Cape. Groups of Sotho spread to the southwest and occupied parts of what is now northwestern Limpopo, while smaller groups of Tsonga and Venda moved into Limpopo province. These groups formed kingdoms and lived by herding and farming.

Clashes occurred in a fight for dominance of the land, causing division within the various kingdoms. Even though there has been extensive cross-cultural mixing among all the races, many of these ethnic divisions still exist today.

COLONISTS

In 1488 the Europeans arrived. A Portuguese mariner, Bartholomew Dias, was the first to discover the Cape of Good Hope. Ten years later, Vasco da Gama, another Portuguese, passed the Cape en route to India.

It was a century later that sailors encountered dark-skinned people when they landed at Western Cape to get fresh water and to barter with the people they met for cattle and sheep for fresh meat. Still South Africa's interior remained largely unknown.

In 1651 the Dutch East India Company sent Jan van Riebeeck to establish a settlement at the Cape. With his wife and 90 weak, scurvy-stricken men, he set out to tame the wilds of South Africa. He erected a fort and a hospital and provided meat and fresh vegetables for passing Dutch fleets.

In the late 1650s, African, Indian, and Southeast Asian slaves were brought to the colony. Under the energetic rule of a new governor, Simon van der Stel, and with slave labor, the colony prospered with good harvests of wheat and the production of wine. Settlers moved inland and started farming the fertile soil.

In 1688 about 150 French Huguenots strengthened the ranks of the farmers. By 1779 the white population had grown to 15,000.

Above: **A slave lodge of the Dutch East India Company is now the History Museum of Cape Town. It houses the tombs of Jan and Maria van Riebeeck, the founders of the city.**

Opposite: **Indigenous people of South Africa.**

23

INTO THE INTERIOR

As the white farmers, known as Boers (BOO-ers), advanced into the interior, they encountered black indigenous peoples who had been emigrating southward. The various groups were divided into kingdoms, each headed by a chief. A chief's wealth was measured by how many farms, people, and herds of cattle he controlled. The Zulus, led by Shaka, were one of the most powerful of these groups. It was Shaka's dream to extend his power to create one united kingdom.

In 1820 some 5,000 immigrants arrived from Britain and were sent to farm in Eastern Cape. The British wanted to increase their influence in the Cape and provide a buffer zone against the Xhosas (KAW-sahs) who were establishing themselves there. When the British started encroaching on Xhosa land, fierce fighting between the two groups broke out.

The great Zulu chieftain, Shaka, negotiating with the Boers.

Many Boers in Eastern Cape felt that they were not being represented by the British and saw no future under British rule. In 1836 Dutch families began crossing the Orange River into the interior. The breakaway farmers were known as Voortrekkers (FOO-ehr-trekkers). Over the next decade, an estimated 15,000 men, women, and children departed for the interior in what was known as The Great Trek.

Many bloody battles with the black indigenous groups ensued, but eventually the Boers defeated the Zulus in 1838 and set up their first republic in KwaZulu-Natal. Four years later, it was annexed by the British. The Boers farther north and west had more success in claiming land for themselves. In 1852 the Transvaal Republic was founded and later the Orange Free State.

THE WAR YEARS

At the end of the 19th century, tension escalated when the Boers refused to grant political rights to the British mining population in Witwatersand. On October 11, 1899, the Anglo-Boer War broke out. The Boers held their ground throughout most of the 32 months of conflict but the British force of nearly 500,000 soldiers proved to be too much. The Boers eventually negotiated for peace and the Treaty of Vereeniging (Fir-EEN-i-GHIN) was signed on May 31, 1902, transforming the Transvaal and Orange Free State republics into British colonies again.

In 1910 the British parliament approved the formation of the Union, making South Africa a self-governing dominion within the British Commonwealth. Louis Botha became South Africa's first prime minister. The republic was based on the parliamentary system, but blacks could only become representatives if they were nominated by whites.

During World War I, South Africa joined forces with Britain and the Allies and drove the Germans out of southwestern Africa (today's Namibia). South African forces also fought in Flanders and in East Africa.

When Botha died in 1919, Jan Christiaan Smuts became prime minister. When World War II broke out, Smuts persuaded the country to declare war on Germany. Starting with only 20,000 soldiers, he managed to assemble 350,000 by 1945.

South African soldiers helped defeat the Italian Army in Ethiopia during the early stages of the war. In 1941 two infantry divisions fought as part of the British Eighth Army in the Sahara Desert. They took part in the courageous stand at the Libyan port of Tobruk, where they almost stopped Germany's famed Afrika Korps.

After the war, Smuts was made field marshal of the British Army. He later became a leading figure in the formation of the United Nations.

Jan Smuts, one of the greatest South African leaders.

25

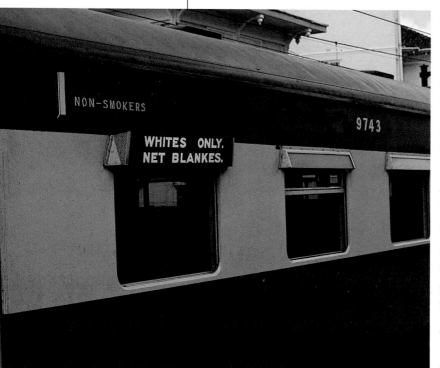

Under apartheid, this first-class train car was reserved not only for nonsmokers but also for whites.

BLACK AND WHITE

In 1948 Smuts was ousted by the National Party led by D. F. Malan, who introduced apartheid to ensure the protection, maintenance, and consolidation of the white minority so as to dominate the black majority.

On May 31, 1961, white South Africa voted for independence from Britain and cut ties with the Commonwealth. That year, Malan's successor, Hendrik Verwoerd, tightened apartheid policy. He was against racial mixing and wanted blacks to live in Homelands separated from the whites.

In protest, the African National Congress (ANC) and the Pan Africanist Congress (PAC) campaigned against the unfair treatment of blacks. The government reacted harshly. Blacks were killed, tortured, and imprisoned, and organizations such as the ANC and PAC were outlawed.

The rest of the world was outraged. Countries such as the United States and the United Kingdom imposed sanctions, bans, boycotts, and restrictions, and severed ties with South Africa. The United Nations made it clear that apartheid would not be tolerated. The South African government responded brutally. Military operations were intensified, all anti-apartheid organizations were banned and many blacks were detained without trial. These measures only served to entrench the unfair policies further.

SOUTH AFRICA TODAY

For three decades, South Africa suffered under the oppression of apartheid. On February 2, 1990, the country's president, F. W. de Klerk, declared that apartheid would be dismantled and the ban on groups such as the ANC lifted. Political prisoners, including ANC leader Nelson Mandela, were freed and most racial laws and restrictions removed.

A negotiating council was formed with representation from all the different political groups and races. An interim government was established and a new constitution developed. In April 1994 all South Africans voted for the country's first ever democratic government. On May 10 that year Nelson Mandela became the first legitimate president of South Africa.

Today South Africa is accepted internationally and admired for the way it has changed and moved forward as a democracy. It has rekindled its relationships with the many countries that had boycotted it in the past and now has diplomatic ties with most countries in the world, most notably China and all the African nations.

South Africans of all races.

South Africa is a member of the African Union, formerly the Organization of African Unity, an international organization that promotes cooperation among the independent nations of Africa. It is active in the New Partnership for Africa's Development (Nepad). This brainchild of five African leaders, including South Africa's Thabo Mbeki, aims to relieve high poverty levels and develop economies in Africa by committing member countries to good governance, respect for human rights, working for peace, and poverty relief.

GOVERNMENT

THE REPUBLIC OF SOUTH AFRICA has a democratic government. After the first elections in 1994, President Nelson Mandela ruled the country for five years in accordance with its new constitution. The African National Congress (ANC) party held the majority in the national and most of the provincial and local governments, but other opposition parties were also democratically represented.

The second fully democratic elections were held in 1999. Again the ANC won the majority of seats across the country. However Mandela decided to step down and Thabo Mbeki took over as the second legitimate president of South Africa.

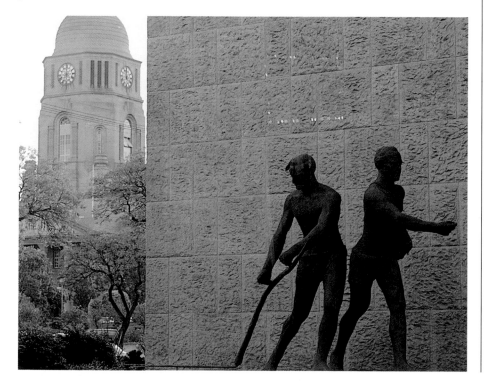

Left: **The Administrative Center in Pretoria.**

Opposite: **The Supreme Court in Johannesburg.**

Parliament House, Cape Town.

NATIONAL GOVERNMENT

The government of South Africa is made up of three separate parts: executive, legislative, and judiciary. The rights of the people are guarded by the constitution. There are three tiers of government: national, provincial, and local.

CONSTITUTION In 1996 South Africa adopted its constitution, which gives every citizen rights and obligations. These are enshrined in the Bill of Rights, which is a body of law that protects every citizen's rights. The constitution is the highest law of the land, and not even the president or parliament can pass a law that goes against the Constitution.

CABINET After elections, the parliament chooses a new president who appoints the deputy president and a minister to head each government department. The president and ministers form the cabinet. It is their responsibility to run the country, but they cannot make laws.

PARLIAMENT The parliament has two houses—the National Assembly and the National Council of Provinces. The constitution says that the National Assembly must have no more than 400 and no fewer than 350 members of parliament (MPs). They are elected through a system called proportional representation, where candidates are elected in proportion to the number of votes the party wins in the election. The president and his ministers are accountable to the parliament. MPs draw up the laws that govern the lives of South Africans and must discuss and debate government policy and other political issues. The parliament makes the laws, but the courts, which are independent of the government, punish the lawbreakers.

NATIONAL ASSEMBLY The National Assembly and the National Council of Provinces debate all the bills that the parliament draws up and can approve, reject, or change them before they are made into law. The National Assembly is also the place where ministers must report on the work they do and answer questions about their work.

One of the chambers where representatives of the South African government meet.

POLITICAL PARTIES AND OTHER POLITICAL ORGANIZATIONS

There are about 18 to 20 political parties in South Africa with about 13 usually represented in the parliament. This number is not constant because there are only three or four larger political parties so the smaller ones often join in order to get a bigger supporter base.

There are electorial rules for all parties, as administered by the Independent Electorial Commission. After the elections, only parties that get 10 percent or more of the vote are eligible to have members in the parliament, the actual number being dependent on proportional representation. The majority vote winner from each constituency also becomes a member of the parliament.

Usually only a few of the larger parties hold most of the seats in the parliament. Despite this, almost all political views from conservative to moderate to liberal are reflected at some level.

AFRICAN NATIONAL CONGRESS (ANC) Formed in 1912, this is the largest and most popular political party. When it was banned in 1960, the ANC embarked on a guerrilla war against the government. The ban was lifted in 1990, when the ANC, represented by Nelson Mandela (*left*) began talks with the white government. Mandela was the party leader during the 1994 democratic elections and became the president of the country.

NEW NATIONAL PARTY (NNP)
Originally this was called the National Party, an all-white organization that ruled under apartheid. It later amended its policies and is now supported by all South Africans, both black and white. This party was led by F. W. de Klerk (*left*), and while he was president, he released Mandela from prison and declared the end of apartheid. Recently, the party changed its name to the New National Party and has entered into an agreement with the ANC to help run the country. In the past these two parties strongly opposed each other.

DEMOCRATIC ALLIANCE (DA) This party was the result of a joining-of-forces between the Democratic Party and the Federal Alliance. Although not very large, the DA sees its role as challenging the ruling party and forming an opposition that speaks up about anything it feels is unjust.

INKATHA FREEDOM PARTY (IFP) The IFP is led by Zulu chief Mangosuthu Buthelezi and is supported by a large number of Zulu people, especially from the KwaZulu-Natal province. It is one of the stronger opposition parties in the parliament.

Other smaller but active parties include the Pan Africanist Congress and the South African Communist Party. There are also a number of the political organizations in South Africa. They are not political parties and are not represented in the parliament, but they have strong support. One such organization is the Congress of South African Trade Unions (COSATU), the umbrella body for all major trade unions in the country.

A campaign poster for Thabo Mbeki during the elections.

THE JUDICIARY Members of the judiciary are not elected but appointed and they function independently because neither the government nor the individual is allowed to interfere in the work of the judiciary. It is the responsibility of the courts to try people who are accused of breaking the law and, if defendants are found guilty, to sentence them to punishment. The Constitutional Court has the power to decide whether the government is acting against the constitution or whether the parliament has made a law that is unconstitutional.

INDEPENDENT ELECTORAL COMMISSION The Independent Electoral Commission was established to control the election process and ensure that every election—national, provincial, or local—is free and fair so that South Africa remains a truly democratic country.

PROVINCIAL GOVERNMENT

THE NATIONAL COUNCIL OF PROVINCES One of the two houses of the parliament, this was created to ensure that provinces and local governments have a direct voice in the parliament when national laws are made. The council consists of delegations from the nine provinces as well as one representing all the local governments.

PROVINCIAL POWERS South Africa's nine provinces each hold joint powers with the central government in matters of national administration and regional autonomy over provincial affairs. Each province has a

SOUTH AFRICA'S NATIONAL ANTHEM

In 1994, when South Africa had its first democratic election, the country had two national anthems. One was *Die Stem can Suid-Afrika,* or The Call of South Africa, from the past ruling party. It was written by C. J. Langenhoven in 1918 and set to music by Reverend M. L. de Villiers in 1921. The English translation was accepted in 1952.

The other anthem, which most people who opposed apartheid used, was *Nkosi Sikelel' iAfrika.* This was written and composed in 1897 by Enoch Sontaga, a Tembu tribesman who was also a teacher. The original version had only one verse, but several more were added in later years.

In 1997 a shortened version of the two anthems were joined together to become the National Anthem of South Africa.

Nkosi sikelel' iAfrika
Maluphakanyisw' uphondo lwayo,
Yizwa imithandazo yethu,
Nkosi sikelela, thina lusapho lwayo.

Morena boloka setjhaba sa heso,
O fedise dintwa le matshwenyeho,
O se boloke, O se boloke setjhaba sa heso,
Setjhaba sa South Afrika—South Afrika.

Uit die blou van onse hemel,
Uit die diepte van ons see,
Oor ons ewige gebergtes,
Waar die kranse antwoord gee,

Sound the call to come together,
And united we shall stand,
Let us live and strive for freedom,
In South Africa our land.

legislature of between 30 and 100 elected members, the actual number based on proportional representation. The local legislatures elect a premier, who heads a cabinet. The size of the cabinet also depends on proportional representation.

LOCAL GOVERNMENT

MUNICIPALITIES Residents of each town or city elect a municipal council that is responsible for running the municipality and providing all the services that make it work, such as garbage collection, water supply, and electricity, as well as running the town or city. About half the municipal councillors are elected directly by the people in the area they serve and the other half are chosen based on proportional representation—in much the same way as it is done for the parliament.

ECONOMY

UNTIL THE END OF THE 19TH CENTURY, South Africa was an agricultural country. The discovery of gold and diamonds triggered a need to invest in mining and machinery. That propelled South Africa into becoming the major industrial power in Africa.

THE MODERN AGE

For most of the 1900s South Africa's economy rode on the back of gold, coal, and other mineral exports. It produced more than half of the world's gold, enabling it to import goods it did not produce. Adequate iron ore and wealth from its gold supply allowed it to establish iron and steel industries. Other industries such as manufacturing, construction, and financial services soon developed. Toward the end of the 20th century anti-apartheid foreign sanctions strained the economy, but democratic change in 1994 opened the world to South Africa's minerals and its wide range of agricultural and manufactured products.

The new government's business policies have helped the economy grow while keeping inflation rates reasonably low. Because South Africa is again a player in the global business environment, it has been able to expand its exports for the benefit of all its people.

Opposite: **A mine worker points to a vein of gold in a Johannesburg mine.**

Below: **The financial district of Johannesburg.**

The central business district in Durban.

COMMUNITY DEVELOPMENT

More and more South Africans are moving from the farms to the towns and cities to work, especially since apartheid was dismantled. This has meant that there is not enough regular housing for everyone, especially for those who are not able to afford a proper place to stay. In an effort to resolve the urban housing shortage the government is building a large number of new houses each year especially for the low-income families.

In the meantime, many people build informal homes on the outskirts of the towns and cities using any scrap material they can find, including wooden planks, metal sheeting, and plastic. Living in informal settlements is not easy, as often there is no running water or electricity and living conditions are very crowded.

As the economy grows and people earn higher wages—and with some help from the government—it is hoped that regular houses will completely replace informal settlements.

RESEARCH

South Africa has a wide variety of plants and animals, a wealth of mineral resources, and a kaleidoscope of ethnic groups. This makes it is a natural laboratory that offers unique opportunities for research. The country's scientists are the technological leaders of the continent, and their work has benefited people and industries throughout the world.

Research in South Africa is funded jointly by the government and businesses. This allows various organizations to conduct research in almost every field.

Major national research centers include the Council for Scientific and Industrial Research (CSIR), which conducts studies in the development of science and technology, the Human Sciences Research Council of South Africa (HSRC), which concentrates on areas such as human resources and education, and the SA Medical Research Council (MRC), whose main aim is to improve national health care.

There are also a number of other research agencies in South Africa. Some are linked to the many universities in the country, which are doing work at an international level in areas such as mining, agriculture, science, housing development, and medicine.

A South African offshore oil platform.

A train goes over a viaduct in South Africa.

TRANSPORTATION

Over the years, South Africa has developed the best transportation network on the continent. Since 1936 highways and roads have connected all the major cities in the country.

Transportation in South Africa is provided by both the government and the private sector. Transnet is a large government-owned corporation that is responsible for all seaports, roads, railroads, and the national airline, South African Airways. It has privatized some of the services in these areas so that now private companies operate a number of the transportation services in the country for both people and cargo.

Private companies build, run, and collect tolls on some roads and are involved in running both passenger buses and heavy cargo trucks. They also operate some terminals in the seaports.

The rich buy their own cars. Those who cannot afford to do so use the minibus taxis, which carry about 12 to 15 people at a time and offer a quick and fairly inexpensive service. Transnet's large railroad network ferries millions of passengers throughout the country each year. It also carries cargo, especially products such as coal and iron ore, to the seaports for export. Some landlocked African countries such as Botswana and Zimbabwe also use South Africa's railroads and seaports to import and export goods.

MANUFACTURING

South Africa has a growing manufacturing industry that is strongest in the metals, chemicals, food, beverages, and building materials sectors. Car manufacture is a large business for both local demand and export.

Manufacturing is responsible for 24 percent of the country's gross national product and accounts for approximately 12 percent of the labor force.

Private enterprise is encouraged, but there is still a substantial amount of government ownership and financial subsidizing in the manufacturing industry. The state-run Industrial Development Corporation (IDC) finances major projects in oil production, phosphate extraction, and the production of pulp for rayon. It also helps to finance manufacturing projects near the Homelands that attract minimal interest and are therefore limited in their potential for growth.

A truck plant.

MINING

Mining makes up 7.5 percent of South Africa's gross domestic product (GDP). Exports of gold, coal, and platinum alone bring in more than US$10 billion a year. The country is the world's largest gold producer, supplies more than half the world's platinum, and is also a very important diamond and coal producer.

Indeed, gold has played an important role in South Africa's economy. When the price of gold skyrocketed in the 1970s, gold mining became an extremely profitable venture. South Africa's principal gold fields are located in Gauteng and Free State. The two provinces also contain large deposits of asbestos, chromium, coal, iron, platinum, tin, and uranium.

The recent rapid rise in the world price of platinum has made platinum mining in South Africa very profitable. The country has large deposits and is expected to be a major producer for many years to come.

Coal accounts for a large portion of South Africa's mining industry. Much of the coal is used locally to generate electricity, but a large quantity is exported.

Uranium, processed as a by-product of gold and copper mining, is exported to countries that use it in nuclear power plants. The first uranium treatment facility in South Africa was established in 1951.

Iron ore, zinc, tin, lead, phosphate,

Workers at the Premier Diamond Mine.

42

and vermiculite are among the other minerals mined in South Africa.

South Africa produces 9 percent of the world's diamonds and has one of the richest diamond deposits in the world. Most of South Africa's diamonds are mined from the ground, but there are good diamond deposits in the oceans and off the country's western coast. At least 90 percent of the diamonds mined in South Africa are exported.

More than 80 percent of the mined minerals are exported. South Africa's exports include 50 different types of commodities, the most important are gold, coal, platinum, diamonds, iron ore, copper, manganese, asbestos, nickel, zinc, tin, lead, phosphate, and vermiculite. The country's huge deposits of iron ore have allowed it to be self-sufficient in the production of steel.

Box cars loaded with quartz being pulled to the surface of a mine.

Despite safety precautions, about 50,000 miners have been killed since the beginning of the 20th century. South Africa mines at depths of 2.4 miles (3.86 km)—deeper than any other country—and has a safety record that is superior to most countries.

South Africa's mining industry provides thousands of jobs. However, the work is very dangerous and the pay is not very high. As a result, many South Africans are reluctant to work in the mining indsutry so mine workers have to be recruited from neighboring states.

Despite abundant mineral wealth, international trade still plays a very important role. The country imports heavy machinery, electronic equipment, and trucks. South Africa is also dependent on foreign nations for oil.

FISHING

South Africa has a strong fishing industry. Its location at the tip of the continent gives fishing boats access to both the Atlantic and Indian oceans, which are teeming with marine life. More than 1,000 varieties of sea creatures, including mackerel, anchovy, herring, and horse mackeral are found off the coasts of South Africa. The Benguela Current, which carries the fish to the north, cuts through the waters to the west where almost 80 percent of the nation's annual catch is made.

Since 1994 smaller companies and individuals have been participating in the fishing industry, which used to be controlled by large companies.

Fishing boats in Cape Town harbor.

TOURISM

South Africa's tourism industry has boomed since positive reports about the post-apartheid South Africa have filtered to the rest of the world. It has become a popular tourist destination.

Visitors to South Africa have a number of options ranging from magnificent beaches to some of the world's most famous game parks and nature reserves. There are massive mountain ranges guarding verdant valleys, vast inland plains, forests, and waterfalls. Many mineral and hot springs can also be found in South Africa.

The nation's controlled tourism industry puts wilderness to work without destroying it. Environmentally conscious tourists will be pleasantly surprised by South Africa's well-preserved natural landscape, and people are flocking to the country for safari tours. To cater to the expanding tourism industry, the government has developed efficient road, rail, and air transportation systems.

Jersey cows in South Africa.

AGRICULTURE

In the past, South African agriculture was run by large-scale farmers. There is now a move to encourage and help small-scale farmers. In this way more people, especially the blacks, are getting involved. The biggest problem for agriculture in South Africa is the lack of enough water in many areas. Only 22 percent of South Africa's total land area is suitable for cultivation.

Corn is the most valuable crop as it is the staple food of the black population. Wheat is grown mainly in the southwest, which receives the most rainfall. Other crops such as oats, rye, barley, tobacco, peanuts, and sorghum are also cultivated but to a lesser extent.

Fruit is the second most valuable crop. Although citrus fruit is not native to South Africa, most varieties are grown successfully. Vineyards are also important to South Africa's agriculture and most are located within a 150-mile (241.4-km) radius of Cape Town. KwaZulu-Natal has been producing large quantities of sugarcane since 1870. Its humid climate makes it suitable for growing subtropical fruit, which can also be found in Mpumalanga province. Dairy products are produced mainly for the domestic market.

Traditional cattle farmers have large herds because livestock is regarded as a measure of wealth. Many traditional farmers are turning to commercial farming, with help from the government and foreign aid organizations that help individuals obtain grazing land. However, the droughts in recent years and a decline in grazing land have taken their toll on cattle farmers.

THE WORKFORCE

A lot of work in South Africa is still not mechanized, meaning that thousands are employed in manual work, especially in the mining and agricultural sectors. Most manual laborers do not have much education and are unskilled or semi-skilled. The government is trying to improve the accessibility and quality of education so that people will be able to do more skilled work in the future.

In the past, most middle- and senior-level people in business and industry were white, while most low-level workers were black. This is changing as new laws ensure that the whole workforce, from company executives to regular workers, is more representative of the entire spectrum of people in the country, most of whom are non-caucasians.

Laws now ensure that women are treated equally in the workplace. The South African government has one of the highest percentages of women in politics and government in the world. The business community is slowly following this lead. Laws are also in place to force companies to employ people of all races if they do not do so willingly.

A South African miner.

A fruit packer.

UNIONS

Since 1924 white trade unions have had extensive and well-defined rights. This did not extend to blacks or their unions until the 1980s. In the 1980s black unions, which tended to be political, became powerful and eventually won full bargaining rights. Before the 1994 elections some of the black and white unions merged.

The new government rewrote labor laws giving workers fair work and pay conditions. Unions now have no race distinction and accept members from almost all economic sectors. Only those working at very top management levels are not allowed to join unions.

There are a number of very powerful unions, especially in the mining, transportation, and automobile manufacturing industries. Recently, with improved work and pay conditions, there are fewer strikes. Unions focus on working conditions, leaving political matters to the political parties. The Congress of South Africa Trade Unions (COSATU) is an umbrella body that unites almost all South African trade unions.

WORKING CONDITIONS

Now that apartheid has been dismantled, South African labor laws have instituted minimum wages, fair working conditions, and good labor practices for all workers in the country. This is especially important for the less skilled, such as farm workers and domestic workers, who in the past were paid very low wages and worked hard for long hours. It also ensures that women are given the same treatment as men.

If workers feel they have been unfairly treated, and especially unfairly dismissed, they have the right to take their case against their employer to the Commission for Conciliation, Mediation and Arbitration, where both parties will be heard and fairly judged.

ENVIRONMENT

IN THE EARLY YEARS of South Africa's colonial history, especially in the 18th and early 19th centuries, very little environmental conservation was carried out. This was mainly because not much was known about the concept at the time. There was so much hunting in the country, not simply as a means of getting food but also for sport, that hundreds of thousands of animals were slaughtered.

As the world changed and saw how the natural environment was being destroyed, leaders in South Africa realized that the conservation of animals and plants and their habitats was essential. For more than a century, South Africa has been actively involved in conserving its abundant natural plant and animal life and original terrain in a wide variety of game parks and conservation areas.

The largest and most famous game park, the massive Kruger National Park, was set up in 1898 to preserve the natural environment of South Africa's Lowveld region. The park spans the low grassland region in Limpopo and Mpumalanga provinces.

Today the government, working through its Department of Environmental Affairs and Tourism, continues the process of environmental conservation. It is constantly updating its policies and approach to conservation in line with world trends. This will enable it to continuously preserve South Africa's natural heritage for all future generations at home and around the world. The government is also working to engage the population in both caring for and living off the country's natural riches without damaging them.

Above: **Women living in a shantytown in Natal, Durban.**

Opposite: **Environmental conservation has helped to ensure that South Africa's natural landscape is not further destroyed by man.**

INCLUDING PEOPLE

Early conservation was done mostly by not allowing the people living near a game park to use it in any way other than paying to visit the park. That led to conflicts because the neighboring communities who lived off the land did not feel part of the process. Poaching and illegal hunting were also persistent problems.

South African National Parks (SANParks) has been entrusted to oversee and manage the country's 20 state-owned national game parks. Its policy follows the modern view that the successful long-term management of the parks depends greatly on the cooperation and support of the local people. Now, parks and communities benefit from each other. For example, the people can sell their handicrafts in the parks so that tourists get a taste of South Africa's art as well as its wildlife.

BIODIVERSITY

Biodiversity, the wide variety of plants and animals and their environments, is considered a national asset as important as diamonds or gold. Environmental conservation is of great importance. There is a lot of pressure on the natural environment from a growing population, farming, deforestation, and other man-made activites. At present there are a number of threatened species of plants and animals that need additional protection.

On a practical level, one of the great advantages of conserving biodiversity is the continuance of many medicines that are made from plants found only in South Africa. Some of the plants are used in modern medical science, while others are used by the *sangomas* or traditional healers, and herbalists.

TRANSFRONTIER PARKS

South Africa shares a few transfrontier, or cross-border, parks with its neighbors. By joining separate parks together, huge wilderness areas can be formed that are better geared for sustainable wildlife conservation and development.

When transfrontier parks are set up, there are no man-made boundaries within them. The animals are able to roam freely and naturally, as they did before people built borders around tracts of land to mark out their respective countries. It also means that visitors to the parks are able to move freely within these very large areas and get a true feeling of what the great wilderness is like.

One of the largest initiatives that South Africa is involved in is the Great Limpopo Transfrontier Park. It joins conservation land and game parks in South Africa to those in Mozambique and Zimbabwe. The park is 13,437.5 square miles (34,803 square km) in size—larger than Israel—and is home to a wide variety of animals and vegetation. Within the park, visitors will also find archeological sites from the Stone Age and Iron Age, evidence that ancient man once roamed the wilderness of South Africa.

Other transfrontier parks and neighboring countries that South Africa is involved in are the Ai-Ais Richterveld with Namibia, the Kgalagadi with Botswana, the Limpopo-Shashe with Botswana and Zimbabwe, the Lubombo with Botswana and Zimbabwe, and the Maloti-Drakensberg with Lesotho.

Above: **The National Botanic Garden of Kristenbosch in Cape Town.**

Above: **Jackass penguins at Boulders.**

MARINE PROTECTED AREAS

Being at the southern tip of the African continent, South Africa has a long coastline—about 1,800 miles (3,000 km) long—and takes great measures to protect it. One such measure is the establishment of marine protected areas (MPAs), which are special areas set aside for protecting either one marine species or a wide variety of marine life. This usually means that no one may fish or interfere in any way with marine life in that area in order to keep it as close to its original natural state as possible. This helps the protected marine habitat and its inhabitants to grow and sustain other creatures that move in and out of the area such as sharks, whales, and dolphins.

MPAs are important because overfishing has reduced the numbers of certain species of marine life to dangerously low levels. Fishermen blame MPAs for bad business, but the government remains committed to protecting the nation's natural resources for future generations. One of the larger and more beautiful MPAs in South Africa is the Tsitsikamma National Park on the eastern coast near Plettenberg Bay.

TOURISM AND ENVIRONMENTAL EDUCATION

South Africa is blessed with a variety of animals and plants and this is one aspect of the country that attracts a growing number of visitors each year. Tourism creates jobs for many people across South Africa, especially near game parks or coastal resorts. Tourism is also very important because it helps generate money to fund conservation.

Conservation can only be really successful when as many people as possible in the country understand what it is about and why it is necessary. Thus emphasis has been placed on teaching young South Africans about their natural heritage. For example SANParks runs programs that expose young people to the wilderness in a national park. It is hoped that they will in turn teach and inspire others in their communities.

There are also private organizations such as the Wildlife and Environment Society of South Africa (WESSA) and The Endangered Wildlife Trust, which help increase awareness and teach people how to make the least possible negative impact on the environment.

South Africa is a founding member of the Antarctic Treaty, which dedicates the area south of the 60° latitude to peace and science. It also provides for the environmental protection and conservation of this important region in the southern ocean.

Left: **Visitors to the game reserve in Ngala watch an elephant in its natural habitat.**

It is not uncommon to find trash strewn at the side of the road in townships.

ELECTRICITY GENERATION

South Africa generates its own electricity mostly from coal. Even though this is the least expensive method, it is also environmentally unfriendly. Eskom, the state-owned power company, is constantly trying to improve the efficiency of power stations while at the same time reducing their pollution levels. It is also exploring more efficient and less polluting means of generating electricity, such as from natural gas.

Some electricity is generated from nuclear power. Wind power and solar energy could also become important sources of electricity in the future.

PLASTIC BAGS

People often jokingly call plastic bags South Africa's national flower because many discarded bags can be found strewn on the roadside in towns and cites. The bags are also found caught on wire fences and in tree branches. To reduce plastic bag litter, the government introduced a law in 2003 forbidding shops to give out plastic bags. Shops can either give out paper bags or sell customers thicker, stronger bags that can be re-used.

WORLD SUMMIT

The United Nations World Summit on Sustainable Development, also known as the Johannesburg Summit because it was held in Johannesburg in August 2002, brought together tens of thousands of people, including heads of state and heads of government, national delegates, and leaders from non-governmental organizations (NGOs), businesses, and other groups. Their aim was to focus the attention of the whole world on conserving Earth's natural resources and improving the quality of life of many millions of people who do not live with the same benefits, such as running water and electricity, good jobs, and enough food, as do people in the United States, Europe, and other countries.

At the summit people from all over the world discussed the problems they faced, the possible solutions that could be found and also what had been achieved and learned in the 10 years since the first summit, the Earth Summit held in Brazil's Rio de Janeiro in 1992. They also discussed how groups, organizations, and countries could help one another, what they could learn from one another, and what could be learned from mistakes made in the past.

Apart from the main summit meetings, there were other fringe events held for a variety of NGOs, trade unions, and other groups as well as for members of the public. The United Nations was the main organizer of the Johannesburg Summit with help from a South African organization, Johannesburg World Summit Company.

SOUTH AFRICANS

THE NEARLY 44.8 MILLION CITIZENS of South Africa represent a spectrum of cultures. At one end is the urban middle class who live a modern, Western lifestyle, a group that has seen an increase in blacks since the end of the apartheid. At the other end are the industrial workers and small-scale farmers, who are generally poor and live in small homes on the outskirts of towns and cities or in the rural areas.

The majority of South Africans—35.4 million—are blacks from different indigenous groups such as Zulu, Xhosa, and Sotho. The whites total 4.3 million and are mainly of Dutch, British, French, German, and Portuguese descent. There are about 4 million mixed-race, or Colored, people and 1.11 million Asians.

Left: **South Africans relaxing outside the Botanical Gardens in Cape Town.**

Opposite: **Zulu warrior**

A young South African black.

BLACKS

Blacks entered the country from the interior of Africa over a period of several centuries. By 1500, a group of blacks called Nguni had occupied the land for centuries. By 1651, when whites began settling in what is now South Africa, they met groups of Sotho-speaking people.

From their first meeting, it was clear that blacks and whites had a different concept of land ownership. Blacks did not regard the land as private property but as a communal possession. Whites, on the other hand, overran large tracts of land in order to better their position and power.

Black indigenous groups were formed through a hereditary system of authority. The Zulus, one of the most prominent groups, was led by a famous leader called Shaka, who ruled the entire region now known as KwaZulu-Natal. The Zulu empire disintegrated after the arrival of the whites. A period of coexistence between the blacks and whites followed but there was no integration.

Before moving to the towns and cities built by the whites, many blacks first established themselves on farms. A large proportion still live in the rural areas on small farms and in villages. The rural areas are often shabby and run-down, and many people are unemployed. Some homes may have no running water or electricity, but the government is trying steadily to improve living conditions. In some cases family members go to work in towns and cities and come home only a few times a year.

NELSON MANDELA

Nelson Rolihlahla Mandela is the most famous South African, known across the world as the leader of the struggle for freedom and democracy in South Africa. Mandela is also known as South Africa's first democratically elected president and as a man who has stood up for justice and fairness for all people around the world, regardless of their race, religion, color, or beliefs.

Mandela was born in a humble village in Eastern Cape province on July 18, 1918 and finished his early schooling there. He completed his first university degree and began studying law when he moved to Johannesburg. At that time he became deeply involved in the struggle of black South Africans for freedom and equality. He joined the African National Congress (ANC), and in  the 1950s he organized campaigns resisting the unfair laws made by the whites. This led to his being tried and convicted for treason, and in 1964 he was sentenced to life imprisonment at Robben Island.

After years of growing resistance from many South Africans and other countries in the world to the unfair and racist policies of apartheid, Mandela was released from prison in 1990 by President F. W. de Klerk. The two men jointly received the Nobel Peace Prize in 1993 for their efforts in ending the apartheid system in South Africa through a peaceful negotiated settlement.

The next year, in the first ever democratic elections in South Africa, Mandela was elected the country's first black president. This was a very meaningful event for a country that had fought against unjust laws for many decades. After his five-year term in office he retired from South African politics. He continues to travel the world, helping peace efforts in other countries. In 2003 he voiced his opposition to the war in Iraq. He has received many international awards and set up the Nelson Mandela Children's Fund.

An Afrikaner couple enjoying the sunshine in a park.

WHITES

The majority of South Africa's 4.3 million whites are descendents of the Dutch, German, French, and British colonists.

AFRIKANERS The origins of this group can be traced to the pioneers of the Dutch East India Company, who settled in South Africa in 1651. By the end of 1750, they had penetrated far into the interior. They were mainly farmers, known as Boers.

In 1814 Britain began its bid for control by trying to Anglicize the 26,000 Afrikaners, but the latter remained steadfast and continued speaking Afrikaans, a simplified version of Dutch, mixed with French and German.

Afrikaners soon became unhappy with British rule. From 1836 to 1838, about 10 percent of the population embarked on the Great Trek. They moved deeper into the interior and founded their own republics, Orange Free State and Transvaal, in the hope of placing themselves out of British reach. Unfortunately the republics were short-lived.

In 1885, the discovery of gold in South Africa brought thousands of fortune-seekers, mainly from Britain. The large influx of British immigrants, combined with the Afrikaners' dissatisfaction with British rule, eventually led to the bloody Anglo-Boer War. After a long campaign, the Boers were eventually defeated, and Afrikaners again came under British rule. In 1910 the Afrikaners regained control of South Africa from Britain.

Afrikaners maintain their distinct identity to this day but also mix with other groups.

ENGLISH-SPEAKING WHITES The British first occupied the Cape in 1795, establishing an English-speaking community.

In 1820, 5,000 Britons arrived at Port Elizabeth and settled on the surrounding land. They brought poetry and prose as well as skills in craftmaking, engineering, and education, contributing to the cultural heritage of the new country. Grahamstown, the center of British influence, grew into a community of learning that boasted several schools and a college. During the 19th century, the British began to penetrate the interior of South Africa, eventually proclaiming Natal as a separate British province. English-speaking South Africans played a big role in the development of the business community, especially in and around Johannesburg.

Schoolchildren enjoying their lunch at Cape Town's Waterfront development.

JEWS   The first Jewish congregation in Cape Town dates back to 1841. Today there are more than 100,000 Jews living in South Africa. Their contribution to economic, educational, and cultural life has been considerable. Jews played a large role in developing the country's business sector, and some were also active in liberal politics pushing for democracy and the end to apartheid. There are synagogues in all of South Africa's large cities, and services are well-attended during Jewish festivals. Johannesburg, Cape Town, and Durban have the largest Jewish populations.

PORTUGUESE   The Portuguese can claim to have been the first white people to set eyes on South Africa. The first explorer to sail around the Cape of Good Hope was Portuguese navigator Bartholomew Dias, who was followed by his compatriot Vasco da Gama on his way to India. Many Portuguese came from Angola and Mozambique after Portugal withdrew from those colonies. In fact, there are about a quarter of a million Portuguese in South Africa, making them the most numerous white minority in the country.

South Africans at a Johannesburg intersection.

ITALIANS   Thousands of Italian soldiers captured during World War II were sent to South Africa as prisoners of war. They were well cared for and were employed on farms or in building and construction companies. After the war, many opted to remain and were eventually joined by their families. They have since added their skills to the food, engineering, textile, and paper industries. Many Italians have opened restaurants, providing South Africans with an authentic taste of Italian cuisine.

GREEKS Large communities of Greeks have settled in all of South Africa's main centers, particularly Pretoria and Johannesburg, where there are Greek churches, schools, and several Greek cultural organizations. About 66 percent of the Greek community have become South African citizens. They range from businesspeople to café or shop owners.

ASIANS

There are 1.11 million Asians living in South Africa, including Indian, Chinese, and other Asian and East Asian people. The majority are of Indian descent, with many coming from India to work on the large sugar plantations of KwaZulu-Natal.

In the Cape Town area, a few thousand Cape Malays, whose ancestors were brought over by the Dutch from Southeast Asia during the colonial period, still form a distinct community. But as South Africans of Asian origin, they are a minority compared to South African Indians and, to a lesser extent, South African Chinese.

A Jewish diamond cutter working on a gem.

The Asian
population was
one of the fastest-
growing groups in
South Africa from
1911 to 1970.

INDIANS Even though the first Indians arrived in South Africa in 1860, it was only in 1961 that they were accepted as a permanent component of South Africa's multicultural population. As a community, Indians are not culturally homogeneous. However, their exposure to Western influences has had a marked effect on their traditional lifestyle. While the older generation continues to observe traditional Asian customs brought over from their home country, the younger generation appears to be adopting a more Western way of life.

South African Indians have had an oppressive and difficult life. They have been discriminated against by successive governments that have designated separate Indian business and residential areas. As it was with the Coloreds and blacks, during apartheid Indians were forcibly removed from certain areas and made to live in designated areas.

The Indian community accepted this unfair treatment but not without protest and court action. They were also active in the ANC and its struggle against apartheid. Being efficient, disciplined, and hard-working businesspeople and traders has helped them greatly in overcoming discrimination. Now that apartheid is a thing of the past, Indians have begun to exercise their freedom of choice in where they live and do business.

Most of the Indian community can be found in and around Durban. There is also a large community in the Johannesburg area as well as in other major cities in the country.

Both the Islamic and Hindu faiths are practiced in the Indian community. In Durban there are some beautiful Hindu temples, and the community participates in the annual Festival of Lights, or Divali. Many of the Indians and much of the Malay community from Cape Town as well as some of the Colored community practice the Islamic faith, worshiping at the many mosques throughout the urban areas in South Africa. They also observe the Islamic holy month of fasting, Ramadan.

English has become the first language for many Indians in South Africa. A majority of the Indians in South Africa today were born in the country. But, many of them still are able to speak Tamil or Hindi, while some are even adept at speaking Afrikaans.

Indians taking a break on a hot, sunny day.

Above and opposite: **South African Coloreds.**

CHINESE A shortage of black labor in the Johannesburg and Reef gold mines in the late 19th century prompted the recruitment of some 50,000 Chinese workers. They arrived soon after the Anglo-Boer War, but by 1910 most of the miners had been sent home. Others arrived in the years thereafter, and today there are about 12,000 South African Chinese living in the country, the majority in Johannesburg.

The South African Chinese population is generally fluent in English and Afrikaans. Many families, however, still communicate in their regional dialects, the most widespread of which are Hakka and Cantonese.

The Chinese continue to play an increasingly important role in the development of a modern South African society.

COLOREDS

The Coloreds are the mixed descendants of the Khoisan, the blacks, and the European and Asian settlers. More than 65 percent of the 4 million Coloreds live in what was previously known as Cape province. Largely Afrikaans-speaking, over the years they have identified primarily with the white population. During the apartheid era, however, many Coloreds sympathized with the blacks. They showed their support by petitioning to reclassify themselves as blacks and by joining anti-apartheid groups. While Coloreds had been victims of discriminatory laws in the past, they were, unlike the blacks, represented in the former government.

Subcultural groups such as the Griquas are also classified as Coloreds. The Griquas are largely of Khoikhoi-European ancestry and have developed a culture of their own. Religion and a love of sacred music and song are the main characteristics of this dwindling community, which is being assimilated into the Colored population. They have also been the victims of discriminatory laws.

LIFESTYLE

WITH THE DISMANTLING OF APARTHEID South African lifestyles have changed drastically, especially for the blacks. It is estimated that by the year 2020 some 80 percent of blacks will be living in cities. Current government policy is directed at helping non-whites secure employment, in government or the private sector, and get a head start in business.

The whites used to have a privileged lifestyle, but this has changed. Most are finding it harder to get jobs as they have to compete with the whole population, not just other whites. The standard of living for some whites has dropped, while increasing numbers of blacks have improved theirs.

Left: **Shoppers in Johannesburg carrying their parcels.**

Opposite: **South African businessmen reading a newspaper in downtown Johannesburg.**

NON-WHITES

Under apartheid, non-whites were separated from whites.

THE ILLS OF THE LAND

To understand the lifestyle of South Africans, it is necessary to know what life was like during the apartheid years. In 1948 racist laws separated blacks from whites in every sphere of life. They also made a distinction for Coloreds, Indians, and Asians. Notices in many places announced "whites only" or "blacks only." The social and economic life of South Africa was based on such distinctions.

A great deal of discrimination resulted, and the wide gulf that developed was a deterrent to social mixing. Some whites thought that by keeping to themselves they would avoid being overwhelmed by the larger black population. Interracial marriages were forbidden, and each group of people had to live in separate areas. The only place they were allowed to mix was in the workplace, and even there discrimination existed.

Black people were required to carry permits or passes when they entered the city. Millions of blacks were arrested and detained without trial. A host of discriminatory laws were passed forcing blacks to take on menial tasks and live in townships where living conditions were poor.

Anti-apartheid committees formed throughout the world in protest against the maltreatment of South African blacks. In 1960 the death of 69 blacks during a protest march at Sharpeville caused a worldwide outcry. Sanctions and boycotts began in support of South Africa's anti-apartheid groups. But the racist policies continued. Black political groups were banned, their leaders thrown in prison, and the streets were filled with death and destruction. Poverty, misery, and large-scale unemployment overtook the country.

After decades of hardship, the government finally relented. In February 1990 it lifted the ban on all political organizations, released political prisoners, and repealed the bulk of discriminatory laws.

The 1994 democratic government abolished the last of the racist laws and discriminatory policies. Needless to say, there have been problems, including an increase in the crime rate, as blacks and whites become accustomed to their new roles and to living as equals in a "rainbow nation." Most South Africans are optimistic about the future of the country, and whites who were dissatisfied with the situation have emigrated.

During the apartheid years, blacks all over the country were forced to live in townships such as Soweto, where living conditions were poor.

BLACK LIFE

For years, many blacks traveled from the Homelands to the cities to work because of the lack of jobs in their areas. Urban blacks live in townships around major cities in small government-supplied houses or shacks made from wood, iron, and plastic. Townships were created by the white government that were in effect huge ghettos. Resentment against apartheid was particularly strong there as several hundred blacks died in township riots. Soweto, outside Johannesburg, was the most rebellious and notorious township. Today the new government has allocated money to upgrade the townships.

Black and white workers in Pretoria.

In the countryside, most blacks live as they did before the Europeans came, in villages of mud and reed dwellings known as kraals. Various indigenous groups use different architectural styles for their dwellings. For instance, traditional Zulu and Xhosa homes are shaped like beehives and made of mud and grass, while Ndebele huts are usually brightly painted with large geometric patterns. Some rural dwellers wear traditional dress consisting of blankets and skins adorned with bright beads and ornaments. Urban blacks have adopted Western-style clothing.

A Transkei traditional healer or sangoma.

CUSTOMS Although each indigenous group has its own distinct customs, some share similar beliefs. One common custom is ancestor worship, a form of religion that is usually mediated by a traditional healer called a *sangoma* (sung-GAW-mah). A number of indigenous groups, such as the Zulu and Xhosa, are superstitious and believe that supernatural beings, often ancestral spirits, can cause misfortune. Their beliefs are reflected in the strict codes of honor that govern their interpersonal relations and the deep respect they hold for their elders.

Although several groups have retained their traditional culture, traditional dress made of hide and decorated with beads, and traditional rituals many of their customs are disappearing. Living in an ever more global and wired world means that many South Africans are adapting at least some of their lifestyle to new ways.

Ndebele women in front of the dwelling in their kraal.

FUNERALS South African black funerals are unique. Black people form burial societies that collect money from members to ensure that in the event of a death the family will have money to pay for the funeral.

A black funeral is regarded as a social event. Underprivileged communities combine their resources to provide food and drink for people who attend the funeral. At some black funerals there are often as many as 400 to 500 mourners present. Funerals are not somber affairs as mourners usually sing and dance. In the past, funerals were often used as political platforms, and mourners would carry protest signs if the person had died of something related to apartheid.

TOWNSHIPS Black townships developed near the major cities due to the presence of hundreds of black laborers working in the cities. Many of the townships were no more than slums of cramped, substandard quarters without plumbing or electricity. Since 1994 the separated living areas have been scrapped. Today every citizen is entitled to live and own property anywhere in the country. In addition, the government spends a large portion of its annual budget to improve conditions in the existing townships and to build houses for the millions of homeless families.

HOMELANDS In 1961, when Prime Minister Hendrik Verwoerd came to power, he tightened all apartheid policies. Although he wanted blacks to continue working in the white cities and towns, he felt that they should return to their own areas at night. He set aside certain tracts of land that were to be used by indigenous groups and called them Homelands.

In order to implement racial policies aimed at further separating whites and blacks, the government forcibly removed blacks from their homes and ordered them to resettle in the Homelands. Families were uprooted and often separated in the relocation. Blacks had to travel long distances in order to reach the cities where they worked, and many left their families to live in the townships.

The Homelands of the Transkei, Venda, Ciskei, and Bophuthatswana made up 13.7 percent of South Africa's land area yet accommodated more than half the population. The Homelands were plagued by overcrowding, erosion, and poor health conditions.

Zululand, in KwaZulu-Natal.

White South Africans enjoying the beach.

WHITE LIFE

Although there is a variety of cultural groups within the white community, their lifestyles are very similar. Many whites attend church, and most are interested in sports, as either spectators or players. Whites enjoy a relatively high standard of living. Their homes, which are often luxurious, are located in city suburbs. During the apartheid years, Afrikaners held most of the government and civic positions. They also controlled the agricultural sector of the economy. Today, the number of Afrikaners working in these areas have decreased as they now have to compete with a larger number of candidates, including the blacks, for these positions. English-speaking whites dominated the nation's businesses and industries.

ASIAN LIFE

The Malay community originally settled in the Cape Town areas and brought many Malay and Islamic customs with them. They have a good reputation as builders and artisans, although now they work in all areas of the economy and government. The Indian communities are mainly situated in KwaZulu-Natal. They are renowned as business people and often own and run their own businesses.

78

COLORED LIFE

Coloreds are usually compared with the white community as their culture and values are similar. Many Coloreds are Christians, but a growing number are becoming Muslims. Many are skilled artisans, and some have entered government, business, education, and the medical profession.

HEALTH

In the past, health care in South Africa was excellent for whites but basic for the rest of the population, with some areas not receiving any medical care at all. Those living in rural areas often had to walk many miles to the nearest clinic, which was not necessarily well-equipped.

Today South Africa is trying to extend good health-care services to everyone and provide health education that covers all the different needs. This is difficult and expensive. Many state-run hospitals and clinics do not have enough facilities, doctors, or medicine to serve the poorer people who use them, but the government is trying to improve this. Only the wealthy can afford the health care provided by the few private hospitals and clinics. Most doctors prefer to work in the urban areas, so the government has decreed that all newly qualified doctors must spend a year in rural areas to help with the shortages there.

The government provides free health care to young children and pregnant women and runs a national nutrition program that provides food for poorer children in primary schools.

Poverty and a shortage of food have always been a problem in South Africa. The government is taking measures to improve the situation, but it will take a long time. The nation also needs economic growth to create more jobs so that everyone can afford better food and health care.

Some public health care rendered by South African government bodies is free or charged according to the patient's means.

A party of schoolchildren on an excursion to the South African Museum in Cape Town.

EDUCATION

Former education policy discriminated against blacks. State-funded education facilities for whites were very good, but this was not the case for black, Colored, and Asian children. Schools for blacks were the most neglected. Although it was compulsory for all children to attend school from the age of seven to 16, it was often not enforced in black schools. Many children, especially the poorer ones, attended school infrequently or not at all. Today an estimated 98 percent of whites can read and write, but the figure drops to 85 percent for Asians, 75 percent for Coloreds, and not much more than 50 percent for blacks.

Education for all was free in government schools until 1992. Although this helped poorer children, the quality of their education was often inferior. It did not prepare them for any sort of decent job in their adult life.

The government has made it a major priority to improve literacy among

all South Africans. Today every school is open to all races, and attendance is compulsory for nine years. School fees have to be paid in most schools, but the government has introduced a system that subsidizes or forgoes fees for children from families who cannot afford them.

Children are taught in English and one of the other 10 official languages. Previously, they were taught in English and Afrikaans, neither of which was spoken in their homes. This made lessons difficult to understand. Private schools are generally elite and charge high fees.

There are a number of universities and colleges, mostly situated in or near the major towns and cities. Fees have to be paid, but there are scholarships to help the underprivileged. They can also study part-time while they work.

Current policies are geared to an education that will help people get good jobs in future. There is a strong emphasis on science and mathematics, areas that were neglected in black schools under apartheid.

RELIGION

ALTHOUGH NOT ALL are actively practicing, more than 70 percent of South Africans are Christians. These Christians are mostly whites and Coloreds but also include blacks and Indians. Some blacks have adapted Christianity to better fit their needs by merging it with their belief in the power of ancestral spirits. Other major religions in South Africa include Hinduism, Judaism, and Islam. As in many urban societies, a growing number of people do not practice their religion or have no specific religion.

Above: **A traditional healer and his assistants.**

Opposite: **The Lady Grey Historic Dutch Reformed Church**

In the past, Christian values were the main focus in government and the media. Now all other major religions are also represented and frequently addressed in public or state gatherings with a more interdenominational approach. The constitution ensures freedom of worship for all.

South Africa has a rich tradition of worship through music, especially choral music. There are many choirs that sing mostly religious music unaccompanied by any instruments. There are large-scale choral festivals and national choral competitions, which are audible feasts of wonderful rich voices. Choir masters play a very important role, and some are renowned for their composing skills. The African part of the national anthem, *Nkosi Sikilel iAfrika,* which means God Bless Africa, was originally written as a hymn.

Two black Christians dressed for church.

AFRICAN RELIGIONS

Traditional African religion is based on fundamentals such as ancestor worship. However, most blacks today are Christians, and this acts as an important bond for the highly diverse population of South Africa.

At least one quarter of the Christians in South Africa are members of African Christian churches, especially the Zionist Christian Church (ZCC), which joins elements of traditional African beliefs with Christian values. The ZCC, the largest church in the country, has its headquarters at Moria in Limpopo province. The Shembe Church in KwaZulu-Natal is similar as it holds Christian beliefs that are integrated with traditional Zulu rituals.

Black and white missionaries have played a vital role in establishing schools, hospitals, and churches. They have presented Christianity to millions and have proved invaluable in the spiritual support, health, and education of the black population. Missionaries were also among the strongest opponents of apartheid.

CHRISTIAN CHURCHES

A vast majority of South Africans are Christians, and many different denominations are represented in South Africa today.

THE DUTCH REFORMED CHURCH The roots of this church can be traced back to the white settlers from the Netherlands in the early 17th century. The Dutch Reformed Church (DRC) in Africa was set up in 1859 and established orphanages and institutions for the

underprivileged and needy. The Dutch Reformed Mission Church in South Africa was started in 1881 by congregations separated from the DRC in Africa. They originally started a church exclusively for Coloreds and people of racially mixed parentage. In 1962 it declared its membership open to all races, and many white opponents of apartheid joined it.

THE PENTECOSTAL CHURCHES The first Pentecostal churches were established in 1908. The late 1980s saw a drastic increase in the number of worshipers, especially among the blacks. The Apostolic Faith Mission Church is the largest Pentecostal church in South Africa. It played a big part in the Pentecostal movement that has swept across the continent during the last 20 years.

THE ROMAN CATHOLIC CHURCH The influence of the Roman Catholic Church in South Africa began to grow after 1838, when the first resident bishop, Patrick Raymond Griffith, arrived. With the help of two priests, he started missions at Grahamstown, Port Elizabeth, and Uitenhage. When Griffith died in 1862, the Roman Catholic Church had been accepted as part of South Africa's religious establishment.

THE METHODIST CHURCH The first South African Methodist Conference met in Cape Town in 1883 under the presidency of John Walton. Many prominent black leaders are Methodists. The Methodist Church runs children's and old-age homes.

Above: Members of a Zulu church choir.

WESTERN RELIGIONS

The majority of South Africans are Christians, even though a good number of them believe in an adapted form of Christianity or do not actively practice. Most whites practice the Christian faith, although there are also strong Jewish communities, especially in the cities.

THE CHRISTIANS One of the larger Christian groups across the country, in the towns, cities, and rural areas, is the Dutch Reformed Church. Christianity originated from the early Dutch settlers, grew and developed to its current form with the Afrikaners in South Africa. Many followers of the Dutch Reformed Church supported apartheid and did not welcome blacks into their church. That led people who believed in the faith but not in apartheid to leave and form churches that were not racially divided.

The Anglican and Methodist churches are also well supported, often by the English-speaking people. The Roman Catholic and Presbyterian churches have smaller followings in South Africa. A number of charismatic churches became popular from the 1970s onwards. The most popular is the Rhema Church, which has its headquarters in Johannesburg.

THE JEWS Judaism has about 750,000 followers in South Africa. The majority are Orthodox, with a small percentage being members of the United Progressive Jewish community. Jews believe in one God and that a divine kingdom will be established on Earth. Jews to go to the synagogue on the Jewish Sabbath, which lasts from Friday evening to sundown on Saturday.

OTHER CHRISTIAN CHURCHES

THE ANGLICAN CHURCH Anglican membership is the fourth largest of all the established churches in South Africa. Archbishop Desmond Tutu, one of the most recognized and respected Christians in the world, was the first black to be the head of the Anglican Church of South Africa.

THE LUTHERAN CHURCH The growth of the Lutheran Church in South Africa was due mainly to the work of overseas missionaries. In 1966 the Federation of Evangelical Lutheran Churches in southern Africa was established. Today, there is considerable support for mission work done by young South African Lutherans.

THE PRESBYTERIAN CHURCH Presbyterians trace their origins to the second British occupation in 1806. One of their major achievements is the establishment of Indian congregations, started by Joseph Prakasin and Ernest Reim. Among their contributions to society are the Fort Hare University and day-care centers for black and Colored children.

OTHER RELIGIONS

THE MUSLIMS   Followers of Islam are called Muslims. Their holy book, the Koran, is believed to have been revealed by God, called Allah, to the prophet Muhammad. The roots of the South African Muslim community were among the Cape Malays and some of the Indian immigrants. Today there is a much larger and more widespread following with about 650,000 members. They are still predominantly in Cape Town but also in Durban and Johannesburg.

THE HINDUS   Most Hindus retained their religion when they came from India to South Africa and have since contributed to the community of more than 550,000 Hindus in South Africa today. They worship many gods and goddesses, some say as many as 300 million Hindu deities. The more important include Brahma, Vishnu, and Siva.

A mosque in downtown Durban.

SANGOMAS The priests of the indigenous groups serve as voices of great authority. They are said to have spiritual powers that help them remove curses, make predictions, and establish links with ancestral spirits.

Sangomas, more often called traditional healers, deal in all forms of clairvoyance, telepathy, and soothsaying. They also provide herbal medicine. Traditional medicine consists of seeds, dried leaves, roots, herbs, bark, and animal tissue. A good number of Africans use traditional healers and herbal medicine to treat illnesses of both a physical and spiritual nature. It is a very old culture passed down from one generation to another. It takes many years to learn this practice because a healer is expected to know a great deal about the plants and animals—where and how to collect the items needed to make up the medicine—as well as to understand spiritual matters. *Sangomas* are similar to a naturopath in the United States but with a spiritual dimension.

Many Africans believe that certain illnesses or accidents are caused by mythical creatures such as the *impundulu* (im-POON-DOO-loo), a large, white bird that feeds on human blood, and the *tokoloshe* (TAWK-o-LAWSH), a hairy dwarf that plays pranks and creates mischief. Both are equally feared for the misfortune they are believed to cause in villages.

A ceremony involving a *sangoma*.

Sanlam
NO
PEDESTRIANS
BEYOND THIS
POINT
GEEN
VOETGANGERS
VERBY HIERDIE
PUNT
SANLAM

LANGUAGE

SOUTH AFRICA has one of the most diverse populations in the world but does not have one language that is spoken by a majority of the population. The 11 languages recognized by the South African government are English, Afrikaans, Ndebele, Sepedi (Northern Sotho), Sesotho, Setswana, siSwati, Venda, Xhosa, Xitsonga, and Zulu.

Official documents are written in English and Afrikaans, but attempts are being made to incorporate more African languages, especially in schools and the media. There are also a growing number of books, magazines, and other media that are being published in English, Afrikaans, and the nine other languages.

Left: **On some occasions, advertising is done with the help of cars.**

Opposite: **In Cape Town, it is common to find road signs in more than one of South Africa's national languages.**

Soweto women enjoy a picnic and conversation.

THE VARIOUS TONGUES

In South Africa, each ethnic group has its own language. In general, Coloreds speak Afrikaans, but those living in Cape Town can usually speak English as well. Asians speak English as well as their own languages, such as Tamil, Gujarati, Hindi, Cantonese, and Hakka. When talking among themselves, blacks use their own languages, such as Xhosa, Zulu, Tswana, and siSwati. Many blacks use English or Afrikaans to communicate with others. Some, especially those who work in the mines, have also learned Fanakalo, a mixture of English, Zulu, and Afrikaans, which is another way to communicate with those who do not speak their language.

In the past, English and Afrikaans were compulsory in schools, but students are now taught in English and in whichever of the other 10 languages dominant in their area. For instance, students in the Western Cape learn English and Afrikaans while students in KwaZulu-Natal learn English and Zulu.

AFRIKAANS

Afrikaans is one of the country's official languages. It had its beginning in 1651, when the Dutch language was brought to the new colony by settlers. Within 150 years, Dutch was supplanted as the spoken language by a simpler version called Afrikaans. The main part of the Afrikaans vocabulary was derived from Dutch, but Afrikaans includes words and phrases from various African languages as well as Malay, Portuguese, English, French, and German.

Afrikaans is an extremely descriptive language, which has coined a rich variety of new names for plants, animals, and words dealing with farming, hunting, and life in the bush. The names tend to be quite imaginative. For example, the town called Riviersonderend (rah-FEE-er-SAWN-dehr-ENT), translated literally, means river without end. Good day is *goeie dag* (GHWEE-a-DAAGH), and goodbye is *totsiens* (TAWT-seens), meaning until next sight.

In written form, Afrikaans was probably first used in 1795 in a satirical poem during the British occupation of the colony. Great South African poets such as Eugene Marais and Louis Leipoldt helped popularize the language with their well-known works.

Daily newspapers in many of South Africa's national languages are sold by street vendors.

ENGLISH

The first English account of travels into the African interior was the journal of Francis Masson in 1775.

Although the history of the British in South Africa only dates back to 1795, the English language was influenced by indigenous South African languages long before that time. In colonial South Africa, English explorers, naturalists, and scientists who visited the land borrowed many native words to label new things they encountered. These included words to describe flora and fauna, topographical features, and customs.

As the use of English extended across the land, more and more words of diverse origin were added to the vocabulary. A number of English words used commonly in South Africa cannot be understood by English speakers outside South Africa. Examples are bottle store (liquor store), robot (traffic light), *braai* (barbecue/grill), *bakkie* (small truck), biltong (jerky), and spoor (animal tracks).

South African English has also borrowed many words from Afrikaans. *Lekker* (LACK-kir) is a common word that describes tasty food or a particularly fun experience.

Many South Africans regarded Afrikaans as the language of racism and oppression because apartheid was devised and implemented by Afrikaans-speaking governments. For years, the black schools of South Africa preferred to use English as the medium of instruction. Yet despite these negative feelings, many blacks and Coloreds speak Afrikaans better than they do English.

KHOISAN LANGUAGES

The Khoisan languages, a series of soft and forced sounds and clicking noises, are not used much today. They are spoken by the Bushmen, who make up a small community in South Africa. Certain Khoisan words have been incorporated into mainstream South African speech such as *quagga,* the word for zebra, which is derived from one of the major Khoisan languages.

BLACK LANGUAGES

The nine official black languages can be divided into four major language groups: Nguni, Sotho, Tsonga, and Venda. The Nguni, by far the largest group, includes the Ndebele, siSwati, Xhosa, and Zulu, whose languages are mutually understandable but strikingly different. For instance, the Xhosa language has 18 click sounds while Swazi has only 12.

The Xitsonga language is spoken by Tsongas and Shanganas, but it is very different from Nguni, and the two groups do not understand each other easily.

With so many languages spoken within one country, compromises are inevitable. The common tongue used is either a hybrid form of Zulu and Xhosa or a Sotho variation mixed with Zulu.

English is spoken everywhere in South Africa.

ARTS

IN THE LAST 30 YEARS OF APARTHEID, the social and political climate influenced the arts. Protest theater was one way township dwellers expressed their frustration with apartheid, and playwrights such as Athol Fugard and Gibson Kente gave international exposure to the suffering of the blacks.

Today South African theater offers a wide variety, from traditional European to traditional African shows. Much of the best theater is a reflection of the changes in South Africa toward becoming a multicultural country. Theater is varied and can take the traditional form of a play, but often the mix is more vibrant and includes music, dancing, and sometimes even audience participation.

Left: **The Smith Street Natal Play House in Durban.**

Opposite: **South African masks from KwaZulu-Natal.**

MUSIC

The African people have a rich and ancient musical tradition. This is either sung or played on instruments such as drums, reed pipes, and xylophones.

Black music is based on traditional African themes, but recently it has undergone fundamental changes due to Western musical influence. Township jazz, known as *kwela* (KWE-lah) music, has become popular both locally and internationally through groups such as Ladysmith Black Mambazo, which teamed up with singer Paul Simon, and Johnny Clegg and his band Savuka. A number of blacks, notably the Xhosa singer Miriam Makeba, trumpeter Hugh Masekela, and jazz pianist Abdullah Ibrahim, have achieved international recognition. The Soweto String Quartet, a classical group that adds African rhythm to some of its music, has also become well-known around the world.

There are a few classical orchestras in South Africa. Previously, most classical musicians were white, but today there are more black players. A number of classical players and composers, such as Arnold van Wyk and Kevin Volan, have contributed to the international classical style.

In some Afrikaner communities, a type of folk music called *boeremusiek* (BOO-rah-moo-SIK) is popular.

A young Zulu drummer whose home is in the Valley of a Thousand Hills.

VISUAL ARTS

ROCK ART Some of South Africa's greatest art treasures are prehistoric rock art, or petroglyphs, that show lively images of animals, hunting scenes, and rituals. Many of the petroglyphs are at least 2,000 years old. There are about 3,000 rock art sites in the country, and they are protected, which means they may not be touched or damaged in any way.

HANDICRAFTS There is a growing handicraft industry in South Africa, and the more contemporary work includes images of cars or animals made out of wire or tin cans such as coke cans or canned fish tins.

Close-up of a Bushman painting in the Drakensburg Mountains.

MODERN ART In the last decades of the 20th century, more black artists became well-known and began selling their works to galleries and collectors. Their works depicted the hardships and injustices as well as the vibrancy of township life. Recently, artists such as J. H. Pierneef, Walter Battiss, Gerard Sekoto, Helen Sibidi, and Karel Nel have added their styles to the growing mix of internationally known South African art. Some of the pieces reflect, in various ways, the country's social and political issues.

Colorful decoration is typical of Ndebele art.

An example of a Zulu kraal in Joubert Park, near Johannesburg.

INDIGENOUS ART Art produced by the various indigenous groups is very distinct. The Ndebele of Limpopo province are renowned for their brightly colored beadwork, while the Zulus are known for their shields and weapons, intricately stitched and using a combination of hides and feathers. Carved wooden sculptures and beautiful woven cloths are among the traditional African art forms. Age-old handicrafts such as pottery, woodwork, mat-making, basketwork, and beadwork are still popular.

TRADITIONAL ARCHITECTURE

The Zulu homes found in KwaZulu-Natal are easily recognized by their beehive shape. The floor of the home is made of anthill soil, mixed and beaten smooth by the women of the kraal. A mixture of cow dung and water is smeared on the floor to improve its durability. The homes, which are made of dried grass, have no windows and only one arched opening for a doorway. Goat skins and mats make up the furnishing.

The most striking traditional African architecture is that of the Ndebele in southern Limpopo and Gauteng provinces. Graphic designs and intricate patterns are painted in bright colors on the walls of their homes.

101

LITERATURE

South Africa has a wide variety of excellent authors from across its rainbow culture. Many are internationally well-known, such as Nadine Gordimer, who won the Nobel Prize for Literature in 1991, and J. M. Coetzee, who won the British Booker Prize twice, the only person ever to do so and the Nobel Peace Prize for Literature in 2003.

For many years, Afrikaans was scorned as a written medium, but from 1925, when it was finally recognized as an official language, over 10,000 books were published in the language. In order to reach an international market, some Afrikaner authors write in English as well.

There are a number of excellent Afrikaner writers. Andre Brink, a former teacher of literature at Rhodes University, has written many novels, including *A Dry White Season*, which criticizes apartheid.

Playwright Athol Fugard's works have been performed internationally. His plays, particularly *Boesman and Lena* and *Master Harold and the Boys,* have received praise from around the world.

Several English-speaking South African authors have achieved worldwide fame. The late Alan Paton, who wrote *Cry, the Beloved Country*, is still one of South Africa's most famous authors, and Wilbur Smith has publicized African game parks with his novels set in the bush. Nadine Gordimer, who has written many novels, used *Burger's Daughter* and *July's People* to show, through the format of a novel, the evils of apartheid.

EXCERPTS FROM FAMOUS SOUTH AFRICAN BOOKS

"Ah, but your land is beautiful. Cruel and beautiful. A man is destroyed for a small sin of the flesh. For it is not a small sin of the flesh but a great sin against the nation. When you know that you will never look any man or woman in the eyes again, when you know that you will never smile or laugh again, when you know you will never jest again, then it is better to die than to live."

—*Ah, But Your Land Is Beautiful* (1981), Alan Paton

"I remember those who used to live in District Six, those who lived in Caledon Street and Clifton Hill and busy Hanover Street. There are those of us who still remember the ripe, warm days. Some of us still romanticize and regret when our eyes travel beyond the dead bricks and split tree stumps and wind tossed sand."

—*Buckingham Palace, District Six* (1986), Richard Rive, a famous Colored author.
(Coloreds were forcibly removed from the suburb of District Six in Cape Town.)

"Attend my fable if your ears be clean
In fair Banana Land we lay our scene—
South Africa, renowned both far and wide
For politics and little else beside.
The garden colony they call our land
And surely for a garden it was planned,
What apter phrase with such a place could cope
Where vegetation has so fine a scope,
Where weeds in such variety are found
And all the rarest parasites abound,
Where pumpkins to professors are promoted
And turnips into parliament are voted."

—*The Wayzgoose* (1928), Roy Campbell

Some of the first African works were by South African writers such as Thomas Mofolo, Solomon Plaatje, and R. R. Dhlomo. *The Wrath of the Ancestors* (1940), a play by Archibald Campbell Jordan, is the best-known Xhosa work. It depicts the modern black author's exploration of urban life.

Censorship played a significant role in South Africa during the apartheid years. Newspapers, radio stations, and publishing firms were all subject to government control. Under the new government and constitution, the right to freedom of expression and of the press is well guarded. This means there is no unreasonable censorship of the media, literature, and the arts. However, there is control of pornographic material.

LEISURE

THE CLIMATE OF SOUTH AFRICA is ideally suited for many forms of outdoor leisure activity, ranging from sports such as rugby and mountaineering to deep-sea fishing to game viewing in the many parks around the country. The warm climate also encourages picnics and barbecues.

South Africans enjoy cultural performances and the theater. Many of the performances are held outdoors as well.

During the apartheid years, sanctions prevented the country's athletes from participating in international competitions. That is now a thing of the past, and many South African athletes take part in international competitions such as the Olympic Games.

Left: **South Africans playing chess on a giant board in a Johannesburg public park.**

Opposite: **Picnikers at Boschendel, Western Cape province.**

An amusement park by the famous Durban beachfront called the Golden Mile.

LEISURE AND RECREATION

In the past, people of different races were not allowed to mix socially and were forced to live in separate areas. As a result the different races developed different leisure lifestyles. After apartheid was abolished, the races began to mix with one another and people could enjoy whatever leisure activity they chose.

Popular in the townships is the practice of popping into a *shebeen* (sha-BEEN). This is similar to a pub but often less formal; it may even be a room in someone's house. People buy a drink and socialize with their friends.

The church is another popular gathering place, with the choir playing an important social role. Black Christians often get together to form choirs that are very popular in the community. During public choral performances, whole communities will turn up to sing and dance.

For the middle classes leisure time revolves around the family. Weekends are often spent outdoors. Friends and family get together to enjoy a barbecue, called a *braai* (br-EYE), from the Afrikaans word *braaivleis* (br-EYE-flais), or grilled meat. Barbecues take place at home around the swimming pool or at a chosen picnic spot.

South Africans who are more affluent often belong to community organizations such as chess clubs, wildlife societies, and bridge groups. Some families do volunteer work with organizations such as the Rotary Club and the Lion's Club that are found in most cities. Such organizations are popular fundraising and social clubs that help needy communities.

Sailing is a popular sport among white South Africans.

The church also plays a significant role for the affluent. Many have their own community-help societies that render excellent service to the society they live in.

Theater, cabaret, and other live entertainment is popular with the affluent South African audiences, and numerous jazz clubs and live music venues are found in the major cities.

In the wealthier neighborhoods, teenagers and twentysomethings mix freely and easily across the cultural lines, especially since they have been to school together. The younger ones tend to have parties in the family home, while the older ones go out to clubs, movies, and bars.

SPORTS

South Africans are crazy about sports, whether they are spectators or participants. Since the 1994 democratic elections and the lifting of the sports ban, South African athletes have been welcomed back into the international sports world. Soccer, rugby, and cricket are the major international sports played, but almost every warm-weather sport is represented and played at some level.

South Africa has produced many sports stars. Some of the best-known include golfers Bobby Locke, Gary Player, Ernie Els, and Sally Little, tennis stars Cliff Drysdale, Kevin Curran, Wayne Ferreira, and Johan Kriek, and world lightweight boxing champion Brian Mitchell.

Soccer, or association football, is the black national sport. Thousands of black spectators support their favorite teams in the local, African, and international competitions. Most townships have vacant lots or fields where children can kick a ball around. Millions of dollars are spent to improve sporting facilities at black schools.

In 1992 South Africa sent a team to the Olympics for the first time in decades. Runner Elana Meyer won a silver medal in the women's 10,000 meters at Barcelona. Athletics has a large following, and there are about 500 running clubs with memberships in the hundreds of thousands. Long-distance and marathon events are often dominated by blacks. Fun-runs are popular fund-raisers for charity, but more serious runners compete in the many road races and marathons around the country each month. The ultimate achivement is the Comrades Marathon, an ultra-distance, 56-mile (90.1-km) route between Durban and Pietermaritzburg.

A lawn bowling game in progress at a club in Port Edward.

In the past, cricket was a mostly white and Indian summer sport. Now schoolchildren are taking up the game seriously and there are exceptional players of all races on the national team. Rugby, once played mainly by whites and Coloreds, is now also played by all.

Public and private swimming pools are open to all races. Except for a few months during winter, South Africans swim throughout the year.

The annual Cape Argus Pick 'n Pay Cycle Tour hosts an average of 30,000 cyclists from the African continent and around the world yearly. The Tour is 68.4 miles (110 km) long and winds through some of the most beautiful coastal and mountain scenery in and around Cape Town. Johannesburg also hosts a long-distance day race each year.

Since the lifting of sanctions on the country, South Africa has been organizing teams to compete internationally in boxing, golf, hockey, basketball, tennis, swimming, cycling, tenpin bowling, lawn bowling, squash, badminton, gymnastics, and ice skating. A more moderate climate gives South Africans a longer training season than their European and American counterparts.

Expensive hotels line the beaches of Durban, a popular vacation city.

VACATION SPOTS

During the summer holidays most vacationers head for the coast, where there are many beaches to choose from, beginning with the fishing beaches of the south-western coast to Cape Town's beaches to the beaches along the Garden Route, which stretches almost to Port Elizabeth. Along the coastal areas visitors can see whales in Hermanus (HER-ma-NIS), the rare Loerie bird in Knysna (NIZE-na), and ostriches in Oudtshoorn (OATS-HOERN).

In Cape Town, visitors can experience the culture of the Cape Malays, who speak Afrikaans instead of their native Malay, but continue to make their superb spicy food. Visitors to the city flock to restaurants for seafood, especially the famed Cape lobsters. Eating is serious business there. The Victoria and Alfred waterfront development on Cape Town's harbor has restaurants, bars, and shops that never fail to attract large foreign crowds as does the vibrant downtown area, which has many restaurants, pubs, theaters, and music clubs.

Durban's tropical climate draws many visitors to its beaches. International surfing competitions have been held at Durban's North Beach, and the famed Golden Mile is a concrete pavilion running the length of the seafront with water parks and amusements.

Vacationers can also visit Gold Reef City, a replica of Johannesburg during the gold rush days. It has modern entertainment facilities that include roller coasters, carousels, and shows featuring indigenous dancers. One favorite attraction is a cage in a mine shaft that descends into the world-famous Crown Mines, once the largest gold mine in the world.

Another favorite activity is taking the luxury Blue Train from Johannesburg to Cape Town. The train is South Africa's version of the Orient Express and is a hotel on wheels that takes passengers on a 1,000-mile (1,609-km) trip through some of the most scenic landscapes in the country. The train provides first-class meals served with silver on linen tablecloths.

Two hours' drive from Johannesburg is the famous Sun City complex. It has hotels, including the well-known exotic Palace of the Lost City, casinos, and an entertainment resort that has hosted shows by international rock stars. It is the largest man-made tropical paradise in the region.

Inside the world-famous Sun City gambling resort.

111

The Mala Mala safari lodges.

THE GREAT OUTDOORS

Game and nature reserves and conservation areas abound in South Africa. The largest and most famous, at 7,812.5 square miles (20,234.3 square km), is the world-famous Kruger National Park in Mpumalanga province. It has about 150 species of mammals, more than 500 bird species, and many reptiles, amphibians, and fish. Visitors can see more than 140 elephants at the Addo Elephant Park or spot black and white rhinoceroses at the Umfolozo Game Park. The various game reserves offer different kinds of accommodation, from simple village homes to luxurious bungalows. Two of the more luxurious game reserves, located near Kruger National Park, are Mala Mala and Sabi Sabi, where visitors are taken on guided game-spotting drives and served five-star meals outdoors.

Camping is also very popular with South Africans. There are hundreds of well-run campsites at the nature reserves, beaches, and game parks.

TELEVISION

Television was introduced in South Africa in 1976. For years it was controlled by the state-owned South African Broadcasting Corporation (SABC), and programs and pro-apartheid news broadcasts alternated equally between English and Afrikaans. Today the SABC is run as a self-standing business, but it is still under the control of the government. This means that there is at times a pro-government slant in some of its news and programming. It has three channels and broadcasts mostly in English but also has a lot of programming in the other major South African languages. In 1994 an Independent Broadcasting Association was established as a watchdog to ensure unbiased broadcasting and quality programs representing all cultures and language groups in South Africa. There are two private TV stations. There is a pay TV business that offers a wide variety of programs, much like the average U.S. cable TV. The other station, e-TV, is a free channel and a private business that is free of government control.

MOVIES

South Africa's film industry has not been properly developed but the country is gaining international appeal as a good location for making films. The country has a diverse natural landscape that provides many suitable locations for shooting movies. International filmmakers have found that it less expensive to film in South Africa than in places like Australia and Europe. The occasional local film has been made fairly successfully, but most of what is produced are soap operas and dramas for local television.

For years, the Publications Control Board exerted strict control over controversial topics such as pornography, violence, and religion. In March 1995, new laws were ratified to ensure more freedom in the film industry and less censorship of magazines.

The majority of films on the circuit are American, although European films and art-house films are also shown in a fair number of movie theaters in the major cities. Movies are a major form of entertainment for many South Africans, and there are good-quality theaters in all the major towns and cities. The most popular venue for cinemas is inside massive shopping centers, where smaller theaters allow for five or 10 movies to be screened at the same time.

FESTIVALS

SOUTH AFRICA has a wide array of cultural and religious festivals. Since 1994 many public holidays, such as Republic Day, have been cancelled, as they celebrated achievements during the apartheid days and were only relevant to whites. New public holidays have been introduced that are celebrated by all South Africans.

South Africans take great pride in their festivals and are very enthusiastic about these special days.

Opposite: **Gombey dancers from Bermuda participating in the Klein Karoo National Arts Festival.**

Below: **An audience enjoying an African choir's singing during one of the country's many music festivals.**

Above: **Zulus during the Reconciliation Day festivities.**

Opposite: **The Voortrekker Monument in Pretoria pays homage to the Boers on the Great Trek.**

RECONCILIATION DAY

Reconciliation Day was once called Dingaan's Day and, later, the Day of the Vow. The story of its origin lies in the history of the Great Trek.

The Afrikaners set out to explore the interior of South Africa during their Great Trek. When they arrived in KwaZulu-Natal, the stronghold of the Zulu kingdom, they reached an agreement with the great Zulu king, Dingaan, to secure large parts of the province. Dingaan tricked the Afrikaners, and after signing an agreement with their leader, Piet Retief, he ordered them to be killed. The Boers had left their weapons outside the camp and 500 of their people were slaughtered on February 6, 1838.

On December 16 that year, the Boer force fought and defeated

Dingaan's men at the Battle of Blood River, named because the waters turned red from the blood of the 3,000 Zulus killed that day. From then on, December 16 was known as Dingaan's Day. In 1952 the National Party renamed Dingaan's Day as Day of the Covenant which was subsequently changed to Day of the Vow in 1980. The vow referred to is one the Boers made with God that if He helped them against the superior numbers of the Zulus, they would honor the 16th of December every year.

A circle of cast-iron wagons, known as the Blood River Monument, was erected to commemorate the victory of the Boers who, miraculously, did not lose any men during the battle. Once apartheid was abolished, the monument seemed out of place. So in December 1998, Zulu Chief Mangosuthu Buthelezi inducted a new memorial for the Zulu warriors who died that day, across the river from the original monument.

In the new South Africa, the Day of the Vow was changed to Reconciliation Day. Although the Zulus lost, they remember that day in festivities, sometimes in reenactments of the events that had happened. In celebrating Reconciliation Day, South Africans remember those battles and others and remind themselves to strive for peaceful reconciliation and national unity among all of the country's people.

Dancers at the Grahamstown Festival.

FESTIVALS

The number of festivals celebrating the arts is growing in South Africa.

GRAHAMSTOWN ART FESTIVAL One of the country's most important annual cultural events, the Grahamstown Art Festival, takes place over a fortnight in July. The festival features various performing arts. Most of the work shown is new and reflects the changes that have taken place in the country and the mixing and merging of races and cultures. Visitors from across the country and the world enjoy the creative and stimulating atmosphere.

The uniqueness of the town itself contributes to the festival's enormous success. Money that is raised is donated to the art community, and every year several prizes are awarded in the areas of sculpture, opera, music, and ballet. But more importantly, the Grahamstown Art Festival brings together people of all races and ethnicities in a spirit of celebration.

KLEIN KAROO NATIONAL ART FESTIVAL   This festival is held during March and April each year in Oudtshoorn. It began in 1994 and promotes all forms of the arts in Afrikaans, especially the visual and performing arts. Music plays a large role, and the festival even attracts acts from other countries such as the Netherlands, which has a similar language to Afrikaans. The aim of the festival is to take a fresh look at the language and culture of the new South Africa and shake off the negative image of the apartheid era. It is a very successful festival and attracts people from sections of the South African population. It has shown how so many South Africans can put their past differences behind them and move forward through artistic expression.

Afrikaners in traditional Boer dress.

NAGMAAL FESTIVAL   In the olden days, it was difficult for Christians to receive holy communion every week as people lived far away from one another and transportation was slow. Once in three months, large numbers would gather on the grassy square that surrounds the Dutch Reformed Church for religious and social reasons.

Today, it is no longer the huge social gathering that it once was. Only a small number of Afrikaners celebrate this festival to commemorate the past.

A crowd gathers to watch an African dance on New Year's Day.

NEW YEAR'S DAY

New Year's Day festivities in South Africa are no different from those in other countries, except there is no snow as it is the middle of summer in the Southern Hemisphere. Celebrations take place outdoors, with picnics, barbecues, and swimming.

Every January in Cape Town, South Africans celebrate the annual minstrel carnival put on by a group of Coloreds. Thousands of minstrels with their painted faces and brightly coloured costumes and hats stroll through the streets playing their banjos and singing. It is a joyful and fun-filled festival. Like the performers in New Orleans' Mardi Gras the minstrels are grouped in clubs, each with its own unique uniform. The clubs compete for annual prizes.

Some participants call this the Coon Carnival. The word coon does have a negative racial meaning, but some South Africans believe that it is part of their cultural history and prefer to keep the original term. Others feel it is a racist word and call it the Minstrel Carnival.

CHRISTMAS AND EASTER

Christmas and Easter are public holidays in South Africa. Although not all South Africans take note of the religious significance of these days, they are happy to have a day off work.

Christmas celebrations are similar to those in other countries. The one exception lies in the fact that in South Africa, Christmas falls in summer. As such, many South Africans opt for a barbecue outside instead of a traditional indoor meal. Some families attend church, and people spend what they can on special foods, a Christmas tree, and gifts for family and friends.

Easter is celebrated with public holidays on Good Friday and Family Day, which is the following Monday. Some businesses close on the Saturday as well, so many people take a long weekend off. Chocolate Easter eggs are usually hidden for children to find, and hot-cross buns are eaten on Easter Sunday. Most Christians attend church on Easter Sunday.

This African dance troupe is one of the contestants in the International Roodepoort Eisteddfod, an international music competition that used to be held once every two years in October. This competition has since been canceled as other events like the Klein Karoo National Art Festival are more well received.

OTHER HOLIDAYS

Aside from religious holidays such as Christmas and Easter, South Africa has a number of other holidays that mark certain milestones in the country's history.

HUMAN RIGHTS DAY On March 21 in 1960, police killed 69 blacks in Sharpeville near Johannesburg as they took part in a protest demonstration against the oppressive laws of the government at the time. It was seen as a turning point in the fight for freedom from the human rights abuses of apartheid. Today March 21 is celebrated to remember every South African's human rights and to ensure they are never abused again.

FREEDOM DAY On April 27 in 1994, South Africans voted for the first time in the country's history. It was the beginning of democracy for the country.

YOUTH DAY June 16 in 1976 was the beginning of the Soweto riots, when the anger of the township youth and, later, others around the country exploded against oppressive segregated education and against the injustice of apartheid. June 16 honors all the youth who lost their lives in the fight for freedom.

NATIONAL WOMEN'S DAY In 1956 over 20,000 women marched to the government buildings in Pretoria to protest against blacks having to carry identity documents and against the unfair apartheid laws. Today August 9 celebrates the contribution women make to the country and reminds everyone of the difficulties and prejudices many women still face today.

Indian dancers during a Hindu festival in South Africa.

HERITAGE DAY South Africa is made up of many different cultures, languages, and traditions. On September 24, the country celebrates the good that comes from respecting cultural differences and enjoying the cultural wealth they bring to what Nelson Mandela called the Rainbow Nation.

FOOD

SOUTH AFRICA'S FOOD IS AS RICH and varied as its people, combining the finest cuisines of Africa, Europe, and Asia.

GENERAL FOOD PRACTICES

South Africa grows fresh produce, but it is expensive and thus accessible only to the wealthy. Fast food and takeout have influenced people across the cultures, especially those in the towns and cities. Locally produced beef, mutton, pork, chicken, and seafood are also available for the large variety of traditional dishes.

The Cape Malays and Indians still use a wide variety of Eastern spices, while the Afrikaners favor a diet rich in meat and starch. Most city dwellers have adopted a general Western style cuisine, with each immigrant group—Portuguese, Italian, Chinese, and African—adding some of its own traditional cooking concepts and ideas. Poorer communities in the townships and rural areas eat more corn meal dishes, as this is traditional and less expensive. The Italians, Portuguese, Chinese, French, and Greeks have kept to traditional cooking methods, and stores stock many foods and spices essential for these cuisines.

Opposite: **South African shop owner weighing out a bag of curry powder for a customer.**

Below: **Pineapple, one of the many fruits grown locally.**

125

A South African toasting bread over a fire.

TRADITIONAL RURAL AFRICAN CUISINE

Traditional African food that is consumed mostly in the rural villages is simple and quite easy to prepare. Usually it is eaten out of a bowl, using the hands. Children are expected to wait until the adults have finished their meal, but no one goes hungry.

Ground corn cooked with water into a smooth porridge called *pap* (PUP) is the staple food of many South Africans. Grinding the corn was traditionally a woman's job, but today it is often bought ready-ground. Vegetables and herbs are often added to the *pap*, which is rolled into balls and dipped in gravy or eaten with stewed meat. Meat is often used to denote status among members of each indigenous group. Men are usually given the head of the animal, regarded as the best part.

AFRIKANER CUISINE

The traditional Afrikaner meal includes one or more types of meat, potatoes, rice, and boiled vegetables often sweetened with sugar. This style of cooking originated on the farms, where meat was plentiful.

Today South Africans invite friends and family to enjoy a meal of salads, steak, chops, and spicy *boerewors* (BOO-rah-WAWRS), Afrikaans for farmers' sausages, cooked over an outdoor fire. This form of entertaining has spread across the city and town suburbs.

Strips of beef, ostrich, or kudu meat—salted, spiced, and dried in the sun—are an Afrikaans invention that many South Africans love. It is called *biltong*, the equivalent of beef jerky. It is an old Afrikaner staple from the time when it was necessary to have nourishing food that would not spoil during long treks into the country.

Afrikaners have a history of making delicious tarts and baked desserts. Some favorites include *koeksisters* (COOK-sis-ters), strips of plaited dough fried and soaked in syrup, and *asynpoeding* (uh-SAIN-PUH-duhng), vinegar pudding. Another popular treat, often eaten for breakfast, is the *beskuit* (buh-SKATE), or rusk, which resembles a chunk of dried bread and is eaten dipped in coffee.

An Afrikaner cooking a typical breakfast of eggs, bacon, sausages, tomatoes, and potatoes.

OTHER FOOD

The oldest and most typical fare on white South African tables combines the recipes the colonists brought from Europe with the richly spiced and curried dishes of the Cape Malays. *Bobotie* (bu-BOOH-tee), a curried meatloaf topped with milky egg, *sosatie* (sos-AA-ty), which is a kebab, usually of meat and sometimes fish, skewered and grilled, and *blatjang* (BLUT-yung), a tangy chutney made from fruit and used as a condiment instead of ketchup, are local adaptations of foods from both East and West.

As a refreshment, many drink a local tea called *rooibos* (RAW-i-BAWS), made from the dried stalks of a scrubby bush that grows in the south-eastern areas of the country. It contains no caffeine or tannin, is used in baking and fruit punches, and is believed to have health-giving properties.

MELKTERT

14 ounces (400 g) flaky puff pastry
1 egg white
4 cups (1 liter) milk
1 cinnamon stick
4 tablespoons sugar

4 tablespoons all-purpose flour
Pinch of salt
2 tablespoons butter
4 eggs, beaten lightly
Ground cinnamon mixed with sugar

Line an 8-inch (20-cm) pie dish with a thin layer of the puff pastry, and brush lightly with the egg white. Heat the milk and cinnamon stick to just boiling. Mix the sugar, sifted flour, and salt in a bowl, and add the hot milk while stirring. Return the mixture to the pot, and heat at a low temperature until it is thick (about 15 minutes). Remove from the heat, take out the cinnamon stick, and add the butter. Let the mixture cool, then add the beaten eggs, blending well with a spoon. Pour the mixture into the pastry shell, and bake at 450°F (230°C) for 15 minutes, then reduce the temperature to 325°F (165°C) for 15 minutes. Sprinkle with the cinammon and sugar, and serve.

A seafood restaurant in Gold Reef City near Johannesburg.

RESTAURANTS

Competition among South Africa's restaurants is very stiff, and a restaurant cannot survive without maintaining high standards.

With such a mix of cultures, eating out is never dull as restaurants cater to all tastes. A wide range of cuisines—international, fusion, Italian, Portuguese, Chinese, Indian, Malay, and African—is available in the many restaurants in all the major cities.

Some of the country's best seafood can be found along the Natal and Cape coast. Steak houses are popular with locals and are generally inexpensive. South Africans of Italian origin have opened many fine restaurants that are famous for their pasta. The Cape Malays' sweet curried dishes and Durban's hot Indian curries can also be sampled in a variety of restaurants in these areas.

Eating out is one form of entertainment that many wealthier South Africans enjoy, especially those living in cities and towns. With so many choices and a new urban culture that entertains regularly in restaurants, city dwellers dine out a few times a week. That and the increasing number of tourists encourage the range of South African restaurants to grow.

BOBOTIE WITH YELLOW RICE

This is a popular main dish among South Africans. It originated from mixing exotic spices brought by Malay slaves in the mid-1600s with Cape province ingredients, such as mutton or other game meat. *Bobotie* (bu-BOOH-tee) is often served with yellow rice.

1 thick slice of white bread
1 cup milk
Cooking oil
1 clove finely chopped garlic
2 roughly chopped onions
1 tablespoon curry powder
1 finely chopped chili pepper (optional)
2 pounds (1 kg) ground lamb or venison
1/2 cup vinegar
1 tablespoon lemon juice
1 teaspoon brown sugar
1 tablespoon chutney

6 fresh bay leaves
2 slices of orange
2 slices of lemon
3 eggs
3³/₄ cups water
2 teaspoons cinnamon
1 teaspoon turmeric or saffron
1/4 teaspoon salt
2 cups long-grain rice
1 tablespoon sugar
1 cup raisins
1 tablespoon butter

Preheat the oven to 320°F (160°C). Soak the bread, crust removed, in 1/2 cup milk, then squeeze the bread dry. Set aside. Heat the oil in a frying pan. Cook the garlic, onion, and curry powder (and chilli if you are using it) over low to medium heat for two or three minutes. Add the meat, and fry until almost done. Add the bread, vinegar, lemon juice, brown sugar, and chutney, and cook for a minute. Remove from heat. In a pie dish that is 3 or 4 inches deep, place the bay leaves, two orange slices, and two lemon slices on the bottom. Fill the dish with the meat mixture. Beat the eggs and 1/2 cup milk, and pour over the meat. Bake uncovered for 30 minutes until the egg and milk form a custard on top of the meat. To make the rice, bring the water, cinnamon, turmeric or saffron, and salt to a boil in a saucepan. Then add the rice and stir. Cook for 20 minutes over medium-high heat before adding the sugar and raisins. Simmer for another 20 minutes, then add the butter and stir well.

KLAPPERTERT

This coconut tart is a popular dessert among South Africans.

1½ cups water
1½ cups sugar
3 cups finely grated fresh or desiccated coconut
6 tablespoons unsalted butter, cut into small bits
2 eggs and an additional egg yolk, lightly beaten
⅛ teaspoon vanilla extract
2 tablespoons smooth apricot jam
1 baked short-crust pastry pie shell
8 strips candied citrus peel, 1 inch long and ⅛ inch wide
Whipped cream (optional)

Preheat the oven to 350°F (175°C). Mix the sugar and water in a saucepan, and bring to a boil over high heat, stirring until the sugar dissolves. Boil the mixture until you can take some out and almost make a soft little ball. Do not stir while it is boiling. Take the pan off the heat, add the coconut and butter, and stir until the butter has melted. Let the mixture cool to room temperature, then mix the egg and vanilla, and vigorously beat into the mixture. Melt the apricot jam over very low heat, stirring constantly, then brush it evenly over the bottom of the baked pie shell. Pour the coconut mixture into the pie shell, spreading it smoothly. Bake for about 40 minutes. Filling should be firm and golden brown. Before serving, arrange the thin strips of candied peel in a pattern on the pie top. Serve it at room temperature, with whipped cream if you choose.

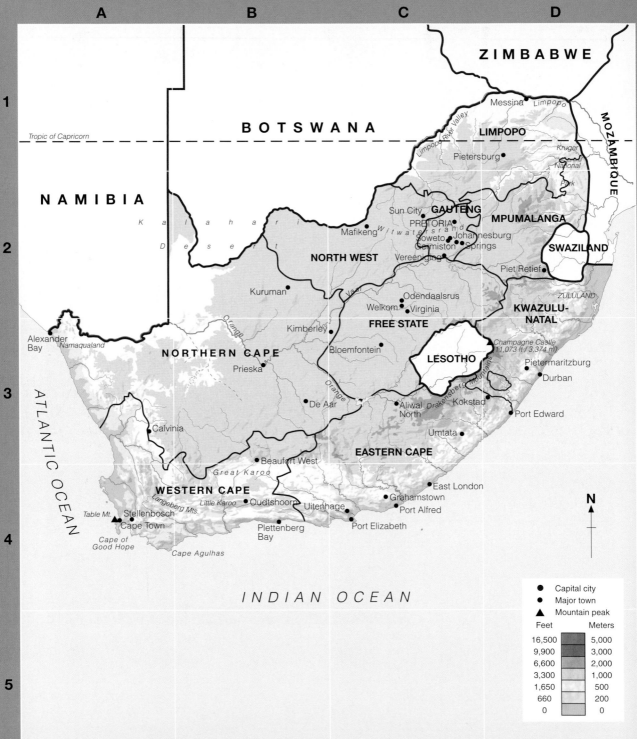

MAP OF SOUTH AFRICA

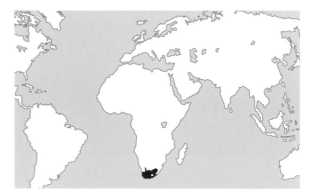

ECONOMIC SOUTH AFRICA

Services
- ✈ Airport
- Finance
- Port
- Tourism

Manufacturing
- Automobiles
- Chemicals
- Textiles

Natural Resources
- Coal
- Diamonds
- Gold

Agriculture
- Cattle
- Coffee
- Corn
- Fruit
- Nuts
- Sheep
- Sugarcane
- Vineyards
- Wheat

ABOUT THE ECONOMY

OVERVIEW
In 1994 the newly elected government set strict, sound economic principles to increase economic growth. The rate of inflation, once very high, has been decreasing, while wealth is beginning to be shared more equally across a larger section of the population. Nevertheless, there is still a lot of potential for economic growth.

GROSS DOMESTIC PRODUCT (GDP)
US$432 billion (2002 estimate)
Per capita: US$10,000

GDP SECTORS
Agriculture 4.4 percent, industry 28.9 percent, services 66.7 percent (2001)

AGRICULTURAL PRODUCTS
Beef, corn, dairy products, fruit, mutton, poultry, sugarcane, vegetables, wheat, wool

INDUSTRIAL PRODUCTS
Automobiles, chemicals, chromium, fertilizer, gold, iron, machinery, platinum, steel, textile, metals

CURRENCY
1 South African rand (ZAR) = 100 cents
USD 1 = ZAR 7.10 (September 2003)
Notes: 10, 20, 50, 100, 200 rand
Coins: 1, 2, 5, 10, 50 cents

LABOR FORCE
17 million

LABOR DISTRIBUTION
Agriculture 30 percent, industry 25 percent, services 45 percent (1999 estimate)

UNEMPLOYMENT RATE
40 percent (2003 estimate)

INFLATION RATE
5.5 percent (2004 estimate)

MAJOR TRADE PARTNERS
Germany, Italy, Japan, the United Kingdom, the United States

MAJOR EXPORTS
Chromite, coal, diamonds, fruit, gold, iron, manganese, platinum, steel, uranium, vegetables

MAJOR IMPORTS
Electronic equipment, heavy machinery, motor vehicles, oil

PORTS AND HARBORS
Cape Town, Durban, East London, Mossel Bay, Port Elizabeth, Richards Bay, Saldanha

AIRPORTS
727 total; 143 with paved runways (2002 est.)

COMMUNICATIONS MEDIA
Telephone: more than 5 million operating main lines; 7.06 million mobile cellular phones (2001)
Internet: 3.07 million users (2002)

CULTURAL SOUTH AFRICA

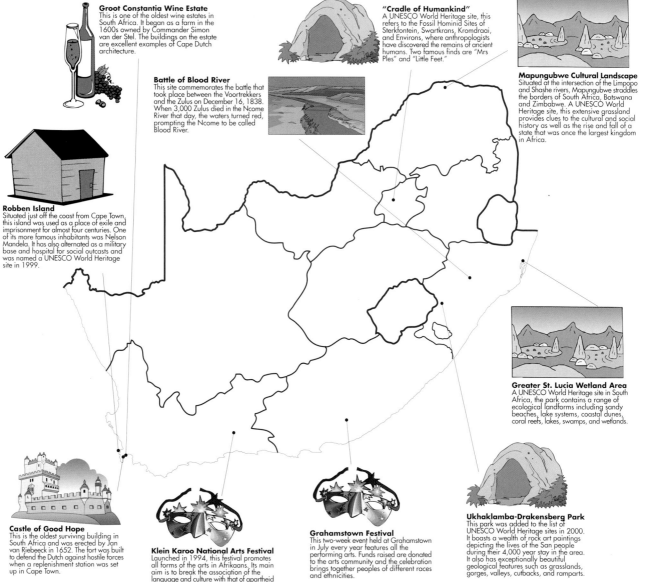

Groot Constantia Wine Estate
This is one of the oldest wine estates in South Africa. It began as a farm in the 1600s owned by Commander Simon van der Stel. The buildings on the estate are excellent examples of Cape Dutch architecture.

"Cradle of Humankind"
A UNESCO World Heritage site, this refers to the Fossil Hominid Sites of Sterkfontein, Swartkrans, Kromdraai, and Environs, where anthropologists have discovered the remains of ancient humans. Two famous finds are "Mrs Ples" and "Little Feet."

Mapungubwe Cultural Landscape
Situated at the intersection of the Limpopo and Shashe rivers, Mapungubwe straddles the borders of South Africa, Botswana and Zimbabwe. A UNESCO World Heritage site, this extensive grassland provides clues to the cultural and social history as well as the rise and fall of a state that was once the largest kingdom in Africa.

Battle of Blood River
This site commemorates the battle that took place between the Voortrekkers and the Zulus on December 16, 1838. When 3,000 Zulus died in the Ncome River that day, the waters turned red, prompting the Ncome to be called Blood River.

Robben Island
Situated just off the coast from Cape Town, this island was used as a place of exile and imprisonment for almost four centuries. One of its more famous inhabitants was Nelson Mandela. It has also alternated as a military base and hospital for social outcasts and was named a UNESCO World Heritage site in 1999.

Greater St. Lucia Wetland Area
A UNESCO World Heritage site in South Africa, the park contains a range of ecological landforms including sandy beaches, lake systems, coastal dunes, coral reefs, lakes, swamps, and wetlands.

Castle of Good Hope
This is the oldest surviving building in South Africa and was erected by Jan van Riebeeck in 1652. The fort was built to defend the Dutch against hostile forces when a replenishment station was set up in Cape Town.

Klein Karoo National Arts Festival
Launched in 1994, this festival promotes all forms of the arts in Afrikaans. Its main aim is to break the association of the language and culture with that of apartheid and allow South Africans to put the past behind them. It is held during March and April each year in Oudtshoorn.

Grahamstown Festival
This two-week event held at Grahamstown in July every year features all the performing arts. Funds raised are donated to the arts community and the celebration brings together peoples of different races and ethnicities.

Ukhaklamba-Drakensberg Park
This park was added to the list of UNESCO World Heritage sites in 2000. It boasts a wealth of rock art paintings depicting the lives of the San people during their 4,000 year stay in the area. It also has exceptionally beautiful geological features such as grasslands, gorges, valleys, cutbacks, and ramparts.

ABOUT THE CULTURE

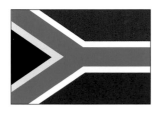

OFFICIAL NAME
Republic of South Africa

NATIONAL FLAG
The colors reflect the four major political parties and combines with a distinctly African character. The broad green stripes flowing into one symbolize the convergence of the past and future.

NATIONAL ANTHEM
National Anthem of South Africa, combining *The Call of South Africa* (*Die Stem van Suid-Afrika*) and *Nkosi Sikelel iAfrika*

CAPITAL CITIES
Pretoria is the administrative capital, Cape Town the legislative capital, and Bloemfontein the judicial capital.

OTHER MAJOR CITIES
Durban, East London, Johannesburg, Pietersburg, Port Elizabeth

ADMINISTRATIVE DIVISIONS
Eastern Cape, Free State, Gauteng, KwaZulu-Natal, Limpopo, Mpumalanga, Northern Cape, North West, Western Cape

POPULATION
44.8 million (2003)

ETHNIC GROUPS
Asians, backs, Coloreds, whites

LIFE EXPECTANCY
46.56 years (2003 estimate)

INFANT MORTALITY RATE
60.84 deaths per 1,000 live births (2003 estimate)

LITERACY RATES
Asians 85 percent, blacks 50 percent, Coloreds 75 percent, whites 98 percent

NATIONAL HOLIDAYS
New Year's Day (January 1), Human Rights Day (March 21), Good Friday (March/April), Family Day (Monday after Easter Sunday), Freedom Day (April 27), Workers Day (May 1), Youth Day (June 16), National Women's Day (August 9), Heritage Day (September 24), Day of Reconciliation (December 16), Christmas Day (December 25), Day of Goodwill (December 26)

LEADERS IN POLITICS
F. W. de Klerk, Nelson Mandela, Desmond Tutu

LEADERS IN THE ARTS
Walter Battiss, Karen Nel, J. H. Pierneef (art); J. M. Coetzee, Athol Fugard, Nadine Gordimer, Alan Paton, Wilber Smith (literature); Ladysmith Black Mamabazo, Miriam Makeba, Arnold van Wyk, Kevin Volan (music)

LEADERS IN SPORTS
Brian Mitchell (boxing); Ernie Els, Bobby Locke, Gary Player (golf); Kevin Curran, Cliff Drysdale (tennis)

TIME LINE

IN SOUTH AFRICA	IN THE WORLD
circa 8000 B.C. San peoples depict objects and events in rock painting in the Drakensberg region.	
circa 1000–800 B.C. Bantu peoples spread through sub-Saharan Africa.	**753 B.C.** Rome is founded.
	116–17 B.C. The Roman Empire reaches its greatest extent, under Emperor Trajan (98–17).
A.D. 300 Early Iron Age farmers lay the foundations of South Africa's mining industry.	**A.D. 600** Height of Mayan civilization
	1000 The Chinese perfect gunpowder and begin to use it in warfare.
1488 Portuguese sailor Bartholomeu Dias lands on South African soil.	**1530** Beginning of trans-Atlantic slave trade organized by the Portuguese in Africa.
	1558–1603 Reign of Elizabeth I of England
1652 Dutchman Jan van Riebeeck sets up refreshment port at what is now Cape Town.	**1620** Pilgrims sail the *Mayflower* to America.
1688 French Huguenot refugees arrive and settle at the Cape.	**1776** U.S. Declaration of Independence
	1789–1799 The French Revolution
1820 The British arrive.	
1835 The Great Trek begins.	
1838 Boers defeat the Zulus and set up the first republic in KwaZulu-Natal.	**1861** The U.S. Civil War begins.
1899 The Boer War starts.	**1869** The Suez Canal is opened.

IN SOUTH AFRICA	IN THE WORLD
1910 The Union of South Africa is formed, with General Louis Botha as first the prime minister.	**1914** World War I begins.
1919 Botha dies; Jan Christian Smuts takes over.	
	1939 World War II begins.
	1945 The United States drops atomic bombs on Hiroshima and Nagasaki.
1948 Smuts is ousted by the National Party led by D. F. Malan, who introduces apartheid.	**1949** The North Atlantic Treaty Organization (NATO) is formed.
1955 Hendrik Verwoerd succeeds Malan and tightens apartheid policy.	**1957** The Russians launch Sputnik.
1961 White South Africa severs ties with Commonwealth and becomes a republic.	**1966–1969** The Chinese Cultural Revolution
	1986 Nuclear power disaster at Chernobyl in Ukraine
1990 F. W. de Klerk declares apartheid dismantled and the ban on groups such as the ANC lifted.	**1991** Break-up of the Soviet Union
1994 The first democratic elections; Nelson Mandela becomes president.	
1996 The Constitution of South Africa is adopted. The Truth and Reconciliation Commission is established.	**1997** Hong Kong is returned to China.
1999 The second democratic elections; Thabo Mbeki becomes president.	**2001** Terrorists crash planes in New York, Washington, D.C., and Pennsylvania.
2003 The Truth and Reconciliation Commission hands its final report to the government.	**2003** War in Iraq

GLOSSARY

Afrikaans
The language of the Afrikaners, closely related to Dutch and Flemish.

apartheid (a-PAHRT-hate)
A policy of racial segregation and discrimination in South Africa before F. W. de Klerk's presidency; originally an Afrikaans word meaning separation.

Boer (BOO-er)
"Farmer" in Afrikaans.

boeremusiek (BOO-rah-moo-SIK)
Music played by an Afrikaans band.

braaivleis (br-EYE-flais)
Meat grilled over the a fire.

fynbos (f-AY-n-BAWS)
A term that describes more than 25,000 plant species indigenous to South Africa.

Homelands
Tracts of land set aside by the apartheid government for non-whites to live on.

Khoisan (koi-SAN)
A nomadic indigenous group.

kraals
A indigenous settlement.

kwela (KWE-lah)
Funky jazz music that originated in the black townships.

Ndebele (ng-de-BEE-leh)
An African indigenous group.

pap (PUP)
A porridge made from ground corn.

rooibos (RAW-i-BWAS)
Local tea made from dried stalks of a scrubby bush that grows in the southeastern regions.

sangoma (sung-GAW-mah)
A medicine man.

segregation
The separation of people according to their ethnic group or race.

shebeen (sha-BEEN)
An illegal drinking house where homemade beer is brewed and served.

townships
Black settlements that sprang up on the outskirts of cities during the apartheid years when blacks and whites were forced to live separately.

veld
Open country with grassy patches.

Voortrekkers (FOO-ehr-trekkers)
The first group of Boers who ventured into the South African interior; from the Afrikaan word meaning front trekkers.

Xhosa (KAW-sah)
One of the Nguni groups.

FURTHER INFORMATION

BOOKS

Chimeloane, Rrekgetsi. *Whose Laetie Are You?* Roggebaai: Kwela Books, 2001.

Hilton-Barber, Brett and Lee R. Berger. *The Official Guide to the Cradle of Humankind*. Cape Town: Struik Publishers, 2002.

Holland, Heifi and Adam Roberts (ed). *From Jo'burg to Jozi*. London: Penguin, 2002.

Lottering, Agnes. *Winnefred and Agnes*. Roggebaai: Kwela Books, 2002.

Malam, John. *The Release of Nelson Mandela (Dates with History)*. Minnesota: Smart Apple Media, 2003.

Mandela, Nelson. *The Illustrated Long Walk to Freedom (Illustrated and Abridged Ed)*. New York: Little Brown Company, 2001.

Pampallis, John. *Foundations of the New South Africa* (New Ed). Cape Town: Maskew Miller Longman (Pty) Limited, 1991.

Paton, Alan. *Cry, the Beloved Country*. New York: Scribner, 1995.

Worden, Nigel, et al. *The Chains That Bind Us: A History of Slavery at the Cape*. Cape Town: Juta and Company, 1996.

WEBSITES

African National Congress. www.anc.org.za

Banknotes of South Africa. www.banknotes.com/za.htm

Central Intelligence Agency World Factbook (select South Africa rom the country list). www.cia.gov/cia/publications/factbook

National Department of Agriculture (NDA). www.nda.agric.za

Nobel e-Museum: Nelson Mandela Biography. www.nobel.se/peace/laureates/1993/mandela-bio.html

Parliament of South Africa. www.parliament.gov.za

Policy and Law Online News. www.polity.org.za

South Africa: Alive With Possibility (official internet gateway). www.safrica.info

South African Government Department of Environmental Affairs and Tourism. www.environment.gov.za

South Africa Government Online. www.gov.za

South African Indian Collections. http://scnc.udw.ac.za/doc/Coll/SAINDCOL.htm

South Africa Missions in New York. www.southafrica-newyork.net

South African National Parks (SANParks). www.parks-sa.co.za

The World Bank Group (type South Africa in the search box). www.worldbank.org

VIDEOS

Cry Freedom. Universal Studios, 1987.

Serafina. Walt Disney, 1992

BIBLIOGRAPHY

Hughes, Libby. *Nelson Mandela: Voice of Freedom.* New York: Dillon Press, 1992.

Miesel, Jaqueline. *South Africa at the Crossroads.* Highland Park, New Jersey: Millbrook Press, 1994.

Pascoe, Elaine. *South Africa: Troubled Land.* New York: Franklin Watts, Inc., 1992.

Paton, Jonathan. *The Land and People of South Africa.* New York: Harper Collins Children's Books 1990.

Smith, Chris. *Conflict in Southern Africa.* New York: New Discovery Books, 1993.

Thompson, Leonard M. *A History of South Africa.* New Haven, Connecticut: Yale University Press, 1992.

Embassy of South Africa in The Hague, Netherlands. www.zuidafrika.nl/default.htm

South Africa Arts and Culture. www.southafrica-newyork.net/consulate/arts.htm

South Africa Government Online. www.gov.za

South African Government Department of Environmental Affairs and Tourism. www.environment.gov.za

South African Reserve Bank. www.reservebank.co.za

South African worship music. www.worship.co.za/pages/za.asp

South Africa's National Holidays. http://africanhistory.about.com/library/bl/blsaholidays.htm

Truth and Reconciliation Commission. www.doj.gov.za/trc/index.html

World InfoZone South Africa Information. www.worldinfozone.com/country.php?country=SouthAfrica

INDEX